S0-BRV-387

WILLIAM WORDSWORTH

First published in Great Britain in 1999 by Brockhampton Press
a member of the Hodder Headline Group
20 Bloomsbury Street, London WC1B 3QA

ISBN 1-86019-9712

A copy of the CIP data is available from the
British Library upon request.

Designed and produced for Brockhampton Press
by Keith Pointing Design Consultancy.

Reprographics by Global Colour
Printed in Singapore.

Image of William Wordsworth on page 4
courtesy of AKG London

WILLIAM WORDSWORTH

A BIOGRAPHY WITH SELECTED POEMS

ROSANNA NEGROTTI

BROCKHAMPTON PRESS

LONDON

WILLIAM WORDSWORTH

WILLIAM WORDSWORTH was born in the small market town of Cockermouth, in Cumberland, on April 7 1770. In his long autobiographical poem *The Prelude,* he states that he felt 'much favoured in his birthplace,' and early sections of *The Prelude* evoke the freedom which Wordsworth enjoyed in his early years, roaming the countryside 'till the daylight failed,' and even then, staying out longer to enjoy the adventure of the night:

> ...at last,
> When all the ground was dark, and twinkling stars
> Edged the black clouds, home and to bed we went,
> Feverish with weary joints and beating minds.

There were five children: Richard was the eldest, followed by William, then Dorothy, John and Christopher. Dorothy was only a year younger than William, and until the death of their mother, they were inseparable. They spent their early childhood wandering together through the countryside, impervious to time, space, distance. 'It is to be noticed,' writes E.E. Reynolds (in Macmillan's 1954 edition of *The Prelude*), 'how far afield Wordsworth roamed even at an age we should now regard as too young for such vagabondage.' Wordsworth writes of how he and Dorothy chased butterflies together, and of playing down on the banks of the river where he apparently 'bathed naked as a savage.' As the biographer Hunter Davies concludes, 'For a conventional, middle-class family of the times, which employed a nurse to look after the children and at least one maidservant, William was allowed a remarkable amount of freedom.' His

RYDAL WATER

mother seems to have despaired of him: she apparently believed, William later recalled, that he was destined for great things, though 'either for good or evil.' The idyll of his early childhood did not last. William's last glimpse of his mother was through her bedroom door, as she lay on her death-bed. Describing his feelings on her death, Wordsworth wrote, 'She left us destitute.' He was eight years old.

Two months later, in June 1778, Dorothy was sent away to live with relatives in Halifax: William didn't see her again for nine years. William stayed on in Cockermouth for another year with his father John, then he was sent to boarding school in Hawkshead, a small town near Windermere. He lodged with a woman called Dame Tyson, who was kind to him, though his lifestyle became somewhat more frugal. At the age of nine, he seemed to be expected to manage his own 'little weekly stipend', sometimes supplemented by a bit of extra pocket money from his father:

> ...we lived
>
> Through three divisions of the quartered year
>
> In penniless poverty. But now to school
>
> From the half-yearly holidays returned,
>
> We came with weightier purses, that sufficed
>
> To furnish treats more costly than the Dame
>
> Of the old grey stone, from her scant board supplied.

More importantly however, William seemed to be allowed the same amount of freedom that he had enjoyed at Cockermouth. He also saw his father during the holidays, as did his brothers. It was a different story for Dorothy, as she reminisced in her journal, 'For six years...I was never once at home, which I cannot think of without regret...' She was often shuttled to her grandparents in Penrith, where she felt tormented, misunderstood and completely alone. In a letter to her friend Jane Pollard, she says of her grandmother:

...while I am in her house I cannot consider myself at home. I feel like a stranger. You cannot think how gravely and silently I sit with her and my grandfather. You would scarcely know me, you are well acquainted that I

was never remarkable for taciturnity, but now I sit for whole hours
without saying anything except that I have an old shirt to mend...

From an early age, the isolated Dorothy became a prolific writer.
She confined herself however to writing letters and keeping journals. Her
writing was concentrated, focused. She could evoke a mood, a scene, a
thought or a feeling in just a few short lines. The following entry in her
journal is simply written, yet Dorothy's sense of depression is palpable
through her deadpan choice of words:

> I was...on the whole, not being well, in miserable spirits. The sunshine, the
> green fields and the fair sky made me sadder; even the little, happy sporting
> lambs seemed but sorrowful to me. The pile wort spread out on the grass a
> thousand shining stars. The primroses were there, and the remains of a few
> daffodils. The well, which we cleaned out last night, is still but a little muddy
> pond, though full of water.

Yet writing for publication would have been out of the question: for
women, at that time, it was not an option. Dorothy's talent brought to bear
instead on William's literary development, and her influence cannot be
underestimated. *Daffodils*, Wordsworth's most celebrated poem, was based
on one of Dorothy's experiences which she logged in her journal. And as
early as 1866, the unnamed W.R. described Dorothy in terms of William as
'the star of his destiny.' Writing in his introduction to Routledge's
second edition of Wordsworth's *Poetical Works*, W.R. continues:

She was not only the blood relation, she was even more than a kindred spirit - she was an inspiring influence. I will even venture to say that to her he owes most of the levation and depth of his poetry: his own genius might have confined him to the metaphysical, to the poetry of the pretty, the little, the odd; it was hers that raised it to the deeply-feeling, the beautiful, and the sublime.

William was certainly struck by Dorothy's sensitivity: it often

DOROTHY WORDSWORTH

appeared almost uncontrollable, and sometimes even he was taken by surprise. When Dorothy 'first heard the voice of the sea, and beheld the scene before her, she burst into tears...This fact was often mentioned among us as indicating the sensibility for which she was so remarkable.' Thomas De Quincey remarked on her mad, staring eyes, which often intimidated strangers. 'At times,' he said, 'the self counteraction and self baffling of her feelings even caused her to stammer.'

In 1783, John Wordsworth, William's father, lost his way in bad weather. He was riding home to Cockermouth from Broughton-in-Furness, and was forced to spend the night out on the slopes of Cold Fell. It was freezing cold, and he returned home feverish. William and his brothers returned home for their Christmas holidays to discover their father mortally ill. He died on December 30 1783, aged 42. When John died, he was owed nearly £5000 by his employer, Sir James Lowther. Lowther was a wealthy, if somewhat corrupt landowner. At one point he had control of nine Parliamentary seats. John Wordsworth acted as his agent, and Lowther was his main client. With this huge debt outstanding on John's death and no other funds, their father's possessions had to be sold. The amount raised was £225, which the five children had to live on whilst waiting for the money from Lowther to come through. It took many years and a series of legal proceedings to achieve this, which meant that for the rest of his childhood, William and his siblings lived on the edge of poverty. Though the boys stayed on at Hawkshead, there was no extra money for luxuries at Dame Tyson's. Dorothy continued to live down in Halifax. Nobody pitched in with

WINDERMERE AND LANGDALE PIKES

any offer of financial help for the children, and Dorothy said later that it was 'mortifying to my brothers and me to find that amongst all those who visited at my father's house he had not one real friend.'

With both parents dead, there was no 'home' as such for the five children: no place to reunite for Christmas or birthdays, nowhere for them to gather together as a family. Although William and Dorothy were apart for nine years, they wrote regularly, and their separation seems only to have consolidated their desire to be together. These letters are often emotionally excessive, and rather more than what you might expect from the correspondence between two siblings. Dorothy would often focus candidly on her feelings. She wrote to her friend Jane, 'I must be blind, he cannot be

GRASMERE LAKE

so pleasing as my fondness makes him. I am willing to allow that half the virtues with which I fancy him endowed are the creation of my love...' William reciprocated Dorothy's frankness - her simple, explicit declarations of affection with their undertone of undying love. One letter to Dorothy reads, 'Oh my dear, dear sister with what transport shall I again meet you, with what rapture shall I again wear on the day in your sight. I assure you so eager is my desire to see you that all obstacles vanish. I see you in a moment running or rather flying to my arms.'

Dorothy never married, and not because she didn't get any offers. Thomas De Quincey claimed William Hazlitt was so enchanted with her that he asked her to marry him: she turned him down. And an obscure reference in one of her letters suggests that the abolitionist William Wilberforce was also keen, having made her acquaintance at a school she had set up for poor children. Hunter Davies concludes somewhat abruptly, 'Dorothy was a virgin - of that there is little doubt.' She seems to have spent her early years anticipating settling down with William as soon as possible. When William left school and went up to St John's College, Cambridge, he found his course dull, having to study a variety of subjects including Mathematics, Classics and Foreign Languages. He was never particularly motivated, even after he chose to study the 'modern' authors of the time. Poor Dorothy patiently waited for him to complete his Tripos, and busied herself making clothes for him to wear whilst he was at the University. When William left Cambridge (he graduated with a poor degree), he seems to have been at a loss. He spent four months in London, with no income: no details are known of where or

SUNSET AT RYDAL WATER

how he lived. Travelling to Wales, he climbed Snowdon in the dark with his friend Robert Jones. Wordsworth remained reluctant to join the clergy (the most obvious option in the early nineteenth century), since he didn't see the point of 'vegetating on a paltry curacy.' Increased family pressure and the offer of a curacy in Harwich through a distant cousin seems to have almost worn down his resistance, and William went back to the Cambridge he found so uninspiring, to learn Hebrew and Oriental languages. He seems to have been preparing for a clerical life. Then, in November 1791, when William should have been in the middle of his first term at College, his friend William Matthews received the following despairing, but ultimately chirpy letter:

I am doomed to be an idler throughout my whole life. I have read nothing this age, nor indeed did I ever. Yet with all this I am tolerably happy; do you think this ought to be a matter of congratulation to me or no? For my own part, I think certainly not. But away with this outrageous egotism. Tell me what you are doing, and what you read. What authors are your favourites and what number of that venerable body you wish in the red sea? I shall be happy to hear from you. My address, Mon, Mons? W. Wordsworth, Les Trois Empereurs, Orleans....

We don't know why William decided to go to Orleans. Perhaps because a Miss Helen Maria Williams was living there, who was a well-known writer at the time; William had long admired her work. His first published sonnet was called *On seeing Miss Helen Maria Williams weep at a Tale of Distress,* and we know that before he set sail from Brighton, he had been given a letter of introduction from what Hunter Davies describes as 'a local literary lady.' Whatever Wordsworth's reasons for choosing to go to Orleans, what was to happen to him in this random French town would mark him in some way for the rest of his life. Curiously, he makes no mention of it in *The Prelude,* and though the facts were known to Dorothy and other members of the family, it was only after Wordsworth's death that the full extent of all that had happened to him came out.

He studied French with a French Catholic girl called Annette Vallon, who was staying in Orleans with her brother. Annette became pregnant. She was twenty-five - four years older than William. In October 1792, William left her and went to Paris: we don't know why. Annette was heavily pregnant, and it would have been very dangerous for an Englishman to be in the French capital. The King had been deposed following the storming of the Tuileries in August, and the following month, the Commune led the September Massacre, where over three thousand royalist sympathisers were taken out of prison and publicly murdered. In late December 1792, William arrived home, and confessed the affair to Dorothy. He wanted to return and marry Annette, but war between France and England broke out and travel became impossible. Dorothy started to write to Annette, and in fact she maintained a more regular correspondence than William. Annette now had a baby girl, Caroline, born December 15 1792. William did not see Caroline until she was nine years old, shortly before he married Mary Hutchinson, an old family friend. After that, he saw neither Annette nor Caroline for another eighteen years...

Different critics read different things into William's liaison: some see him as callous, leaving Annette alone to give birth so that he could witness the extraordinary events in Paris. Others see him as trying to do the right thing: to get back to England and discuss it with his family, and through them to secure more money or a job so that he could marry and support Annette. Most importantly, the critics fight over to what extent the affair 'formed' William as a poet. Herbert Read believes it was crucial, stating, 'Nothing happened comparable in importance with this love affair. It transformed his being; I think that this passion and all its melancholy aftermath was the deepest experience of Wordsworth's life - the emotional complex from which all his subsequent career flows in its intricacy and uncertainty...'

NEAR THE TOP OF STYHEAD PASS, WASTDALE

THE VALE OF ST JOHN, NEAR KESWICK

Another commentator, C.H. Herford, takes a different view. He states flatly that it was possible for Wordsworth, 'without insincerity, to regard it as a passing episode, a moment of tumult that left no permanent trace upon the depths of his poetic thought and feeling.' The truth is probably somewhere between the two. I prefer the pragmatic E.E. Reynolds' take on the whole saga of Annette, warning readers, 'How far this passion influenced Wordsworth's subsequent development is clearly a matter of opinion. Our knowledge of the facts is far from complete, and it is necessary to guard against allowing the imagination to paint a too highly coloured picture.'

A.S. Byatt looks to the poetry William was writing as to some kind of insight into his mind, particularly the following poem in one of Wordsworth's notebooks. It's a strange piece, possibly the only verse Wordsworth ever wrote which was overtly sexual. And whilst it must, most obviously point to Annette, the absent mother of his child, some critics, including Byatt, also suggests that its nuance of guilt and horror may in fact be referring to a fledgling incestuous relationship with Dorothy: short-lived. After William returned from France, he and Dorothy (together at last) moved into a cottage at Alfoxden. It was in one of these notebooks that the poem was discovered:

> Away, away it is the air
>
> That stirs among the withered leaves:
>
> Away, away, it is not there,
>
> Go, hunt among the harvest-sheaves.
>
> There is a bed in shape as plain
>
> As from a hare or lion's lair
>
> It is the bed where we have lain
>
> In anguish and despair.
>
> Away and take the eagle's eye,
>
> The tiger's smell,
>
> Ears that can hear the agonies
>
> And murmurings of hell;
>
> And when you there have stood

By that same bed of pain,

The groans are gone, the tears remain.

Then tell me if the thing be clear,

The difference betwixt a tear

Of water and of blood.

What's clear is that Annette's importance lies with the fact that, for the first time in his life, William had to consider the consequences of his actions, even if he didn't seem to take responsibility for them. We will never know whether his decision to leave Annette was due to the uneasy political situation or his own fears. Annette may, or may not, have had a significant influence on the young poet. Ten years later he married Mary Hutchinson: he was thirty-two - four months older than his bride. There doesn't seem to have been much of a courtship: the impending marriage suddenly appears as a subject in Dorothy's letters. Dorothy herself seemed pleased, 'I have long loved Mary as a sister,' she wrote to her old friend Jane. 'I look forward with perfect happiness to this connection...' Her journal tells a different story. The night before the marriage ceremony, she slept with William's wedding ring on her finger. And in the morning, when it was time to go to the church, she found herself unable to leave the house...

At a little after 8 o'clock I saw them go down the avenue towards the church. William had parted from me upstairs. I gave him the wedding ring - with how deep a blessing! I took it from my forefinger where I had worn it the whole of the night before. He slipped it again onto my finger and blessed

ALFOXDEN

me fervently. I kept myself as quiet as I could but when I saw the two men

[Mary's brothers] running up the walk, coming to tell us it was over, I could

stand it no longer and threw myself on the bed where I lay in stillness, neither

hearing or seeing anything, till Sarah came upstairs to me and said 'They are

coming.' This forced me from the bed where I lay and I moved I knew

not how straight forwards, faster than my strength could carry me,

till I met my Beloved William and fell upon his bosom...

William's marriage to Mary has always been considered somewhat

OLD LABURNUMS AT NEWBY BRIDGE; WINDERMERE

sedate, and centred on a kind of mutual affection. They'd known each other all their lives. In lots of ways, it was the first 'respectable' thing William had done, though Mary's relatives still cut her off when the marriage went ahead. One of them described William as a 'vagabond'. The conventional view amongst critics is that for William, it was a marriage of convenience: William needed a wife, and Mary was also a good companion for Dorothy - they had grown up to be best friends. After the wedding, the three of them continued to live together. It also seems possible that, despite her friendship with Mary, Dorothy never really accepted the marriage. On their 32nd anniversary, she wrote in her journal, 'We let it pass unnoticed. I have again had the resolution not to go out, beautiful as the weather was...'

In 1977, so-called love letters between William and Mary turned up for auction at Sotheby's. A stamp dealer in Carlisle had bought them as scrap for £5, hoping to find some postage stamps. Beth Darlington in *The Love Letters of William and Mary Wordsworth* claims these letters throw new light on the relationship, and reveal the couple as being ardently in love. This is not necessarily the most obvious conclusion. Mary writes far more often than William, and her prattling, inane letters are both desperate and hopeful: 'My dearest William, I sent off a letter to Jane Green yesterday & have yet received none from you since you left Coleorton...' William's more occasional letters are peppered with apologies, claiming not to have received half the letters she sent - probably because he had other things on his mind and couldn't be bothered to keep up the correspondence. Despite his claims to the contrary, it seems likely that he was glad to get away. He enjoyed his walking tours: De Quincey calculated that in his life William had probably walked about 180,000 miles. And though William would often write to Mary of how he was bored and exhausted, he was always somehow able to find excuses not to return home. This example, intended as some kind of justification for his absence, is particularly stunning:

DOVE COTTAGE

My stay at Windsor was longer than I intended by two days; the one, Saturday, I gave as an act of generosity, and the other as I was obliged to give, as it would have been indecent to have left a Clergyman's house on a Sunday, without necessity.

The general consensus is that Wordsworth's emotional life was formed through his relationship with his sister and his lover, Annette: Mary came later, and seems to have been more of a reassuring presence.

But perhaps the most crucial figure in Wordsworth's development was Samuel Taylor Coleridge: S.T.C. to his friends. They met briefly for the first time in Bristol, in 1795, three years after Wordsworth's adventure in France. We don't know a lot about this first meeting, yet in 1797, William and Dorothy moved from Racedown in Dorset to Alfoxden in Somerset, to be near Coleridge, who was living in a cottage at Nether Stowey. The friendship between Wordsworth and Coleridge was intense: they immediately started to collaborate on a poetry collection entitled *Lyrical Ballads*. In 1797, Wordsworth was at the end of a difficult and unhappy time in his life: he was still involved in legal struggles to recoup Lowther's debt. An old family friend had however left William a small inheritance. It was barely enough to live off, though at least meant Wordsworth was released from his dependency on his relatives, and was not forced to take religious orders. Having this money made the world of difference to William: it's a moot point as to whether this small legacy was in fact the most significant thing that had ever happened to him. It freed him up financially, and meant that he had time to write.

Coleridge was a superb speaker: flamboyant and gregarious, he could keep an audience in the palm of his hand, seemingly without even trying. De Quincey claimed to have found more 'weight of truth' in three hours talk with Coleridge 'than would easily be found in a month's select reading.' Yet despite Coleridge's intellectual confidence, he was self-disparaging, inconsistent and unsure of his own worth. His cerebral rigour was offset by a kind of emotional flightiness and unpredictability.

Charles Lamb described him as 'an archangel, a little damaged,' which I find the most moving description. He could undoubtedly be irritating: one of Wordsworth's servants said he was 'a plague' because he demanded cooked meals all the time (Dorothy and William lived off bread and milk: tea was considered a luxury, as were coals for the fire). Samuel Taylor Coleridge was also an opium addict.

In the beginning, Coleridge's easy charm seduced both William and Dorothy. Dorothy described her first impressions of Coleridge in a letter to Mary Hutchinson, William's future wife:

> He is a wonderful man. His conversation teems with soul, mind and spirit.
> Then he is so benevolent, so good tempered and cheerful, and like William,
> interests himself so much about every little trifle.

The letter goes on:

> At first I thought him very plain, that is, for about three minutes: he is pale
> and thin, has a wide mouth, thick lips and not very good teeth, longish,
> loose-growing, half-curling rough black hair. But if you hear him speak
> for five minutes, you think no more of them.

It's worth pointing out that Coleridge also described his first impressions of Dorothy, and the impetus seems to be the same: despite the superlative praise there is an edgy, condemnatory undertow. Perhaps it's because William was the focal point for both their lives, and in a certain sense they had to share him. Coleridge summed up Dorothy as follows, all-too-careful to point out, that though she may be attractive, in no way would you describe her as good looking:

WASTWATER AND SCAWFELL

GRASMERE CHURCH

Wordsworth and his exquisite sister are with me. She is a woman indeed! In mind I mean, and heart; for her person is such, that if you expected to see a pretty woman you would think her rather ordinary; if you expected to see an ordinary woman you would think her pretty! but her manners are simple, ardent, impressive...Her information various. Her eyes watchful in minutest observation of nature; and her taste, a perfect electrometer. It bends, protrudes and draws in, at subtlest beauties and most recondite faults.

Coleridge was as articulate as he was charismatic. He was both a scholar and a performer, blending notions of science, literature and philosophy within the framework of smalltalk. He was also a great enabler, convincing Wordsworth of his own genius, talking at length with him as to the purpose of poetry in a new age, coming up with theories, ideas, possibilities. It was only after spending time with Coleridge that Wordsworth's poetry changed gear. His juvenilia was rigid, over-rhetorical, and a bit stagey. As it developed it somehow became friendlier, more inviting and readable, almost conversational. Reading Wordsworth you sometimes come to feel as though you're having a chat with the poet. It's almost novelistic. As Wordsworth himself stated, 'There is no essential difference between the language of prose and that of metrical composition.' It's this easy, relaxed style that so changed the face of English poetry, breaking away from the stiffer, more formal structures of eighteenth century rhetoric.

This approach was controversial, as was its subject matter, as Wordsworth set in verse portraits from 'low and rustic life': peasants, house-wives, even an idiot boy. This really was quite shocking for poetry readers, as W.R. tells us '...independently of the style being new, Mr. Wordsworth did not choose attractive subjects.' Coleridge tried to help Wordsworth out with his readers, explaining the aim as being 'to give the charm of novelty to things of everyday,' yet the ballad *Alice Fell* was still dismissed by one critic as 'trash.' Yet the simplicity is beguiling. William Hazlitt picked up on the sublimity beneath the surface: he said of the *Lyrical Ballads*, 'Fools have laughed at, wise men scarcely understand them.' Many people were certainly bewildered by them: it was after all, the first time a poet had 'borrowed' the voice of a character–the first time poems had been written where the words emanate from a 'speaker' rather than an 'author'. One reviewer was so confused by *The Last of the Flock*, a poem where the speaker meets a bankrupt man clutching his last sheep, he couldn't understand why Wordsworth didn't lend the man some money. 'If the author be a wealthy man, he ought not to have suffered the poor peasant to part with the last of the flock.' The use of the vernacular confused people. Like reading something in a newspaper, people thought these poems were 'real'.

This early work is day-dreamy, superstitious, occasionally fantastical. The language is vivid, instantly evocative and centred on the natural world. The verse is frequently focused on some recognisable object or *thing*. a thorn, a daffodil, a linnet, starling, stars. Elemental forces infiltrate the poems: the world is as dangerous as it is beguiling. Wordsworth spins stories: his poems tell tales of characters struggling in storms, of wandering children, lost on moors on snowy nights, and of a deserted Indian woman, injured, hungry and alone, waiting to die in the desert. It's as though humans stumble through the world for a short time: we have no permanence, no rock-solidity to our transient presence. We may return as ghosts, wandering rural figures: several of Wordsworth's poems are peopled with spectres, who engage the poet in easy conversation. But the upshot is that for Wordsworth,

WILLIAM WORDSWORTH

the world will continue to spin in its orbit, day follows night as sunshine will follow a storm, and the concrete, unbreakable physical world goes on, unshakable in the time-space continuum.

Wordsworth was in awe of this natural order, of this ongoing history of the world, where a tree is not just a tree but a rooted presence on the horizon, which could theoretically carry on forever. Daffodils will flourish every year, 'Continuous as the stars that shine/And twinkle on the milky way.' A thorn 'stands erect,' growing out of the rock of a cliff, aged but surviving, in spite of being bound... 'With heavy tufts of moss, that

SKELWITH FORCE, LANGDALE

strive/To drag it to the ground.' Most magnificent in its mysteriousness is Wordsworth's description of a yew-tree, 'Which to this day stands single, in the midst/Of its own darkness, as it stood of yore.' This simple, almost stark language has an undertow of mystery and ambiguity from which its richness grows. Coleridge put it better when he said, 'Wordsworth's words always *mean* the whole of their possible Meaning.'

The publication of the *Lyrical Ballads* met with little success. Firstly, the critics were less than rapturous. As Coleridge's wife wrote to him on March 24 1799, 'The *Lyrical Ballads* are not esteemed well here.' Secondly,

William did not make any money from the venture, as he had (rather unrealistically) hoped. The first impression was published in 1798, and described by Dorothy in a letter to their brother Richard as 'one small volume, without the name of the author.' Published anonymously, the work contained poems by both Coleridge and Wordsworth, though Wordsworth's work made up the greater part by two-thirds. Coleridge's epic poem *The Rime of the Ancient Mariner* was however included, though this would come to bring other problems. In Brett and Jones introduction to the 1963 Methuen edition, the authors conclude, 'Things did not run entirely according to plan, but this was because Coleridge failed to keep pace with Wordsworth...'

William thought again about the structure of the collection as a whole, and decided, that the problem was *Ancient Mariner*. He also renamed the book so that it was no longer anonymous: *Lyrical Ballads, by W. Wordsworth*. This seems remarkable given that a few of Coleridge's contributions were still included in the collection. He decided to change things for the second impression, taking *Ancient Mariner* from the its original position at the front of the book and shunting it to the end. He also amended Coleridge's archaic spellings, and wrote what A.S. Byatt has described as an 'ungracious prefatory note,' where he apologised for the poem's 'strangeness.' Though William realised in later years his mistake, and reverted to the original structure of the first edition, the effect this temporary edit had on Coleridge was horrific.

When Coleridge first started spending time with William, his friends worried that he was setting too much store by Wordsworth and his opinions.

Knowing Coleridge's propensity for dependence, his friends were evidently concerned, as the following retaliatory letter which Coleridge wrote to a friend implies:

> You charge me with prostration in regard to Wordsworth. Have I affirmed anything miraculous of him? Is it impossible that a greater poet than any since Milton may appear in our days? Have any *great* poets appeared since him?...Future greatness!

It goes on...

> What if you had known Milton at the age of thirty and believed all you now know of him? What if you should meet in the letters of any then living man, expressions concerning the young Milton *totidem verbis* the same as mine of Wordsworth, would it not convey to you a most delicious sensation? Would it not be an assurance to you that your admiration of the *Paradise Lost* was no superstition, no shadow of flesh and bloodless abstraction, but that Man was even so, that the greatness was incarnate and personal?

Coleridge's unshakable conviction of Wordsworth's greatness almost destroyed him as a poet. After Wordsworth doctored *Ancient Mariner* and then excluded him from the second impression of *Lyrical Ballads,* Coleridge actually stopped writing. 'As to poetry I have altogether abandoned it,' he wrote, 'being convinced that I never had the essentials of poetic genius and that I mistook a strong desire for original power.' He was crushed. 'You would not know me! All sounds of similitude keep at such a distance from each other in my mind, that I have forgotten how to make a rhyme.' Yet, even in this dark time, Coleridge could still pull a stunning image out of the bag, a sparkling metaphor while grieving for his creativity: 'The poet is dead in me–my imagination (or rather the somewhat that had been imaginative) lies, like a cold snuff on the circular rim of a brass candle-stick, without even a stink of tallow to remind you that it was once clothed and mirtred with flame...' Most poignantly, Coleridge wrote:

If I died, and the booksellers will give you anything for my life, be sure

WINDERMERE FROM WANSFELL

NEWBY BRIDGE, WINDERMERE

to say - 'Wordsworth descended on him...from Heaven; by showing to him what true Poetry was, he made him know, that he himself was no Poet.'

Coleridge continued to take opium, prescribed to him as a matter of course from his doctor. Though the substance was medically legal in the nineteenth century, William disapproved, and found himself getting more and more irritated. Coleridge used the drug as a means of inducing a visionary state, and also, as a means of contemplating his own bodily resources, with which he was fascinated. He described pain as a subject which 'exceedingly interests me' whereas William found the drug-taking absurd. He wrote to Coleridge:

> One thing is obvious, that health of mind, that is, resolution, self-denial
> and well-regulated conditions of feeling are what you must depend on;...
> Doctors can do you little good and that doctor's stuff has been one of
> your greatest curses; and of course, ours through you. You must
> know...better than any surgeon what is to do you good...Do not look out
> of yourself for that stay which can only be found within...

Coleridge wasn't interested in listening. He disliked William's preaching tone, stating somewhat sarcastically, 'And I trembled, lest a film should rise and thicken on his moral eye.' As time passed, he became angrier, realising that he wasn't as untalented as he felt Dorothy and William had made him feel with their 'cold praise and effective discouragement.' He perceived their mutual alienation as the Wordsworths' failure to understand

WASTDALEHEAD AND GREAT GABLE

him, writing, 'It is not the Wordsworth's knowledge of my frailties that prevents my entire love of them. No! it is their ignorance of the deep place of my being...' He condemned William as being undeveloped and superficial, of 'living whole among devotees, having every the minutest thing, almost his very eating and drinking done for him by his sister and wife...'

Dorothy had of course taken William's side in the dispute. The factions got worse. Coleridge was in love with Sarah Hutchinson, Mary's sister, and both Dorothy and Mary stopped Coleridge communicating with her, refusing to pass on letters. This aggrieved Coleridge even more. When Dorothy (rather half-heartedly) tried to paper over the cracks for the sake of William, he scorned her invitation to come and visit, stating 'I who for years past had been an ABSOLUTE NUISANCE in the family.' (William had described Coleridge as an 'absolute nuisance' to a third party, and this had somewhat naively been reported back). Dorothy was becoming exasperated, stating in a letter. 'I do not think he can resolve to come if he does not at the same time lay aside his displeasure against William.' But Coleridge was too wounded to ever really come to terms with the editorial fiasco of the *Lyrical Ballads*, stating, 'After 15 years of such religious, almost superstitious idolatry and self-sacrifice - O no! no! that I fear, can never return.'

Wordsworth eventually sent Coleridge a formal apology, seeking to appease what he perceived as Coleridge's touchiness, and a rather impersonal, and carefully worded letter expressing his general regret seems to have worked. They patched it up, though the old intimacy never really returned. Coleridge was more ready to settle their differences as the confidence in his own poetry increased. Wordsworth's poetry in the meantime, lost its edge. In fact, the later work is written in an almost unrecognisable style. Most of the verse in this anthology was written in the first forty years of William's life. He lived to be eighty.

We don't know why the style changed. Many critics feel it was due to circumstances in the poet's life, and that the early works to a certain extent were fuelled by a kind of naivety which became impossible to sustain following the endless traumas to which William was exposed. The death of his brother at sea is often marked as a turning point, as are the deaths of two of his children. The dreaminess of the early work perhaps gave way to the reality of the world, as art for art's sake was replaced by poems which were discursive, opinion-driven and emotionally void. In lots of ways, the early work is about people and their relationship to death, whilst the later work is about life and its relationship to politics. Byron despaired of this shift in subject matter, condemning the extended, philosophical poem *The Excursion* as 'drowsy frowzy' (much to William's annoyance). Wordsworth retaliated by pigeon-holing Byron as a kind of literary flash in the pan, flippantly categorising him as 'a man who is now the rage in London...He wrote a satire sometime since in which Coleridge and I were abused, but these are little thought of...' This glib reply may have reassured the poet's ego, but Byron's poisonous remarks hit their target. In other words, mud sticks. Wordsworth's uneven poetic legacy as articulated by Lord Byron is still being picked over today...

He continued with his walking tours, often crossing Europe by foot. An Englishman ran into Wordsworth and Coleridge in Brussels in 1828, and described Wordsworth as 'tall, wiry, harsh in features, coarse in figure, inelegant in looks.' He said Coleridge looked like a clergyman. Coleridge died in 1834. At his death William wrote to Coleridge's nephew, 'though I have seen little of him for the last twenty years, his mind has been

THE SHEPHERD, YEWDALE, CONISTON

COLERIDGE'S COTTAGE NEAR STOWEY

habitually with me, with an accompanying feeling that he was still in the flesh. That frail tie is broken...' In 1828 Dorothy had some kind of seizure, believed now to be an attack of cholicystitis, with gall stones. She became housebound. Five years later, after a bout of 'flu, her mind noticeably started to degenerate, and within a short time, she became very confused and disoriented. Dorothy spent the last twenty years of her life sitting quietly, gazing blankly into the fire, even in the middle of summer. All those close to William fell away, but he lived on, though his health was a constant source of aggravation. In 1843 he was made Poet Laureate, yet spent the last few years of his life 'tweaking' his existing poetry and chronicling his achievements for posterity. It's surprising to find out that Wordsworth's sight was appalling, and that most of his life he had worn a green shade over his eyes. By the end he was virtually blind and a recluse, dictating notes to Susanna, his nephew Christopher's wife, for use in Christopher's authorized biography. This short, simple document was titled *Autobiographical Memoranda*, and its brief, factual tone is guarded and aloof. It is perhaps coloured by William's grief over the death of another one of his children: his daughter Dora, whom he cherished.

William Wordsworth died on April 23 1850, the anniversary of Shakespeare's birth. Dorothy, an invalid, survived him, though her damaged mind may not even have registered his death. If Blake died singing, Mary offered William other consolations. As he lay dying, she whispered in his ear 'William, you are going to Dora!' He didn't seem to hear, but the following day, barely alive, he whispered to his niece as she entered the room, 'Is that Dora?' He died, we are told, painlessly, surrounded by friends and relatives, as the cuckoo-clock struck twelve.

LUCY GRAY
OR, SOLITUDE

OFT I had heard of Lucy Gray:
And, when I crossed the wild,
I chanced to see at break of day
The solitary child.

No mate, no comrade Lucy knew;
She dwelt on a wide moor,
–The sweetest thing that ever grew
Beside a human door!

You yet may spy the fawn at play,
The hare upon the green;
But the sweet face of Lucy Gray
Will never more be seen.

'To-night will be a stormy night–
You to the town must go;
And take a lantern, Child, to light
Your mother through the snow.'

'That, Father! will I gladly do:
'Tis scarcely afternoon–
The minster-clock has just struck two,
And yonder is the moon!'

At this the Father raised his hook,
And snapped a faggot-band;
He plied his work;–and Lucy took
The lantern in her hand.

Not blither is the mountain roe:
With many a wanton stroke
Her feet disperse the powdery snow,
That rises up like smoke.

The storm came on before its time:
She wandered up and down;
And many a hill did Lucy climb:
But never reached the town.

The wretched parents all that night
Went shouting far and wide;
But there was neither sound nor sight
To serve them for a guide.

At day-break on a hill they stood
That overlooked the moor;
And thence they saw the bridge of wood,
A furlong from their door.

They wept–and, turning homeward, cried,
'In heaven we all shall meet;'
–When in the snow the mother spied
The print of Lucy's feet.

Then downwards from the steep hill's edge
They tracked the footmarks small;
And through the broken hawthorn hedge,
And by the long stone-wall;

And then an open field they crossed:
The marks were still the same;
They tracked them on, nor ever lost;
And to the bridge they came.

They followed from the snowy bank
Those footmarks, one by one,
Into the middle of the plank;
And further there were none!

–Yet some maintain that to this day
She is a living child;
That you may see sweet Lucy Gray
Upon the lonesome wild.

O'er rough and smooth she trips along,
And never looks behind;
And sings a solitary song
That whistles in the wind.

STRANGE FITS OF PASSION
HAVE I KNOWN

STRANGE fits of passion have I known:
And I will dare to tell,
But in the Lover's ear alone,
What once to me befell.

When she I loved looked every day
Fresh as a rose in June,
I to her cottage bent my way,
Beneath an evening-moon.

Upon the moon I fixed my eye,
All over the wide lea;
With quickening pace my horse drew nigh
Those paths so dear to me.

And now we reached the orchard-plot;
And, as we climbed the hill,
The sinking moon to Lucy's cot
Came near, and nearer still.

In one of those sweet dreams I slept,
Kind Nature's gentlest boon!
And all the while my eyes I kept
On the descending moon.

My horse moved on; hoof after hoof
He raised, and never stopped:
When down behind the cottage roof,
At once, the bright moon dropped.

What fond and wayward thoughts will slide
Into a Lover's head!
'O mercy!' to myself I cried,
If Lucy should be dead!'

SKATING BY MOONLIGHT ON WINDERMERE

I TRAVELLED AMONG
UNKNOWN MEN

I TRAVELLED among unknown men,
  In lands beyond the sea;
Nor, England! did I know till then
  What love I bore to thee.

'Tis past, that melancholy dream!
  Nor will I quit thy shore
A second time; for still I seem
  To love thee more and more.

Among thy mountains did I feel
  The joy of my desire;
And she I cherished turned her wheel
  Beside an English fire.

Thy mornings showed, thy nights concealed,
  The bowers where Lucy played;
And thine too is the last green field
  That Lucy's eyes surveyed.

SHE DWELT AMONG
THE UNTRODDEN WAYS

SHE dwelt among the untrodden ways
   Beside the springs of Dove,
A Maid whom there were none to praise
   And very few to love:

A violet by a mossy stone
   Half hidden from the eye!
—Fair as a star, when only one
   Is shining in the sky.

She lived unknown, and few could know
   When Lucy ceased to be;
But she is in her grave, and, oh,
   The difference to me!

CONISTON IN WINTER

NUTTING

————————It seems a day
(I speak of one from many singled out)
One of those heavenly days that cannot die;
When, in the eagerness of boyish hope,
I left our cottage-threshold, sallying forth
With a huge wallet o'er my shoulders slung,
A nutting-crook in hand; and turned my steps
Tow'rd some far-distant wood, a Figure quaint,
Tricked out in proud disguise of cast-off weeds
Which for that service had been husbanded,
By exhortation of my frugal Dame–
Motley accoutrement, of power to smile
At thorns, and brakes, and brambles,–and in truth
More ragged than need was! O'er pathless rocks,
Through beds of matted fern, and tangled thickets,
Forcing my way, I came to one dear nook
Unvisited, where not a broken bough
Drooped with its withered leaves, ungracious sign
Of devastation; but the hazels rose
Tall and erect, with tempting clusters hung,
A virgin scene!–A little while I stood,
Breathing with such suppression of the heart
As joy delights in; and with wise restraint
Voluptuous, fearless of a rival, eyed
The banquet;–or beneath the trees I sate
Among the flowers, and with the flowers I played;
A temper known to those who, after long
And weary expectation, have been blest
With sudden happiness beyond all hope.
Perhaps it was a bower beneath whose leaves

The violets of five seasons re-appear
And fade, unseen by any human eye;
Where fairy water-breaks do murmur on
For ever; and I saw the sparkling foam,
And–with my cheek on one of those green stones
That, fleeced with moss, under the shady trees,
Lay round me, scattered like a flock of sheep–
I heard the murmur and the murmuring sound,
In that sweet mood when pleasure loves to pay
Tribute to ease; and, of its joy secure,
The heart luxuriates with indifferent things,
Wasting its kindliness on stocks and stones,
And on the vacant air. Then up I rose,
And dragged to earth both branch and bough, with crash
And merciless ravage: and the shady nook
Of hazels, and the green and mossy bower,
Deformed and sullied, patiently gave up
Their quiet being: and unless I now
Confound my present feelings with the past,
Ere from the mutilated bower I turned
Exulting, rich beyond the wealth of kings,
I felt a sense of pain when I beheld
The silent trees, and saw the intruding sky.–
Then, dearest Maiden, move along these shades
In gentleness of heart; with gentle hand
Touch–for there is a spirit in the woods.

THE FERRY ON WINDERMERE

CRUMMOCK WATER AND BUTTERMERE

THE LAST OF THE FLOCK

I

IN distant countries have I been,
And yet I have not often seen
A healthy man, a man full grown,
Weep in the public roads, alone.
But such a one, on English ground,
And in the broad highway, I met;
Along the broad highway he came,
His cheeks with tears were wet:
Sturdy he seemed, though he was sad;
And in his arms a Lamb he had.

II

He saw me, and he turned aside,
As if he wished himself to hide:
And with his coat did then essay
To wipe those briny tears away.
I followed him, and said, 'My friend,
What ails you? wherefore weep you so?'
–'Shame on me, Sir! this lusty Lamb,
He makes my tears to flow.
To-day I fetched him from the rock;
He is the last of all my flock.

III

'When I was young, a single man,
And after youthful follies ran,
Though little given to care and thought,
Yet, so it was, an ewe I bought;
And other sheep from her I raised,
As healthy sheep as you might see;
And then I married, and was rich
As I could wish to be;
Of sheep I numbered a full score,
And every year increased my store.

IV

'Year after year my stock it grew;
And from this one, this single ewe,
Full fifty comely sheep I raised,
As fine a flock as ever grazed!
Upon the Quantock hills they fed;
They throve, and we at home did thrive:
–This lusty Lamb of all my store
Is all that is alive;
And now I care not if we die,
And perish all of poverty.

V

'Six Children, Sir! had I to feed;
Hard labour in a time of need!
My pride was tamed, and in our grief
I of the Parish asked relief.
They said, I was a wealthy man;
My sheep upon the uplands fed,
And it was fit that thence I took
Whereof to buy us bread.
"Do this: how can we give to you,"
They cried, "what to the poor is due?"

VI

'I sold a sheep, as they had said,
And bought my little children bread,
And they were healthy with their food;
For me–it never did me good.
A woeful time it was for me,
To see the end of all my gains,
The pretty flock which I had reared
With all my care and pains,
To see it melt like snow away–
For me it was a woeful day.

VII

'Another still! and still another!
A little lamb, and then its mother!
It was a vein that never stopped–
Like blood-drops from my heart they dropped.
Till thirty were not left alive
They dwindled, dwindled, one by one;
And I may say, that many a time
I wished they all were gone–
Reckless of what might come at last
Were but the bitter struggle past.

VIII

'To wicked deeds I was inclined,
And wicked fancies crossed my mind;
And every man I chanced to see,
I thought he knew some ill of me:
No peace, no comfort could I find,
No ease, within doors or without;
And crazily and wearily
I went my work about;
And oft was moved to flee from home,
And hide my head where wild beasts roam.

WILD HYACINTHS

IX

'Sir! 'twas a precious flock to me,
As dear as my own children be;
For daily with my growing store
I loved my children more and more.
Alas! it was an evil time;
God cursed me in my sore distress;
I prayed, yet every day I thought
I loved my children less;
And every week, and every day,
My flock it seemed to melt away.

X

'They dwindled, Sir, sad sight to see!
From ten to five, from five to three,
A lamb, a wether, and a ewe;–
And then at last from three to two;
And, of my fifty, yesterday
I had but only one:
And here it lies upon my arm,
Alas! and I have none;–
To-day I fetched it from the rock;
It is the last of all my flock.'

THREE YEARS SHE GREW
IN SUN AND SHOWER

THREE years she grew in sun and shower,
Then Nature said, 'A lovelier flower
On earth was never sown;
This Child I to myself will take;
She shall be mine, and I will make
A Lady of my own.

'Myself will to my darling be
Both law and impulse: and with me
The Girl, in rock and plain,
In earth and heaven, in glade and bower,
Shall feel an overseeing power
To kindle or restrain.

'She shall be sportive as the fawn
That wild with glee across the lawn
Or up the mountain springs;
And hers shall be the breathing balm,
And hers the silence and the calm
Of mute insensate things.

'The floating clouds their state shall lend
To her; for her the willow bend;
Nor shall she fail to see
Even in the motions of the Storm
Grace that shall mould the Maiden's form
By silent sympathy.

'The stars of midnight shall be dear
To her; and she shall lean her ear
In many a secret place
Where rivulets dance their wayward round,
And beauty born of murmuring sound
Shall pass into her face.

'And vital feelings of delight
Shall rear her form to stately height,
Her virgin bosom swell;
Such thoughts to Lucy I will give
While she and I together live
Here in this happy dell.'

Thus Nature spake–The work was done–
How soon my Lucy's race was run!
She died, and left to me
This heath, this calm, and quiet scene;
The memory of what has been,
And never more will be.

EXPOSTULATION AND REPLY

'WHY, William, on that old grey stone,
Thus for the length of half a day,
Why, William, sit you thus alone,
And dream your time away?

'Where are your books?—that light bequeathed
To Beings else forlorn and blind!
Up! up! and drink the spirit breathed
From dead men to their kind.

'You look round on your Mother Earth,
As if she for no purpose bore you;
As if you were her first-born birth,
And none had lived before you!'

One morning thus, by Esthwaite lake,
When life was sweet, I knew not why,
To me my good friend Matthew spake,
And thus I made reply:

The eye—it cannot choose but see;
We cannot bid the ear be still;
Our bodies feel, where'er they be,
Against or with our will.

'Nor less I deem that there are Powers
Which of themselves our minds impress;
That we can feed this mind of ours
In a wise passiveness.

'Think you, 'mid all this mighty sum
Of things for ever speaking,
That nothing of itself will come,
But we must still be seeking?

'–Then ask not wherefore, here, alone,
Conversing as I may,
I sit upon this old grey stone,
And dream my time away.'

ESTHWAITE LAKE

THE TABLES TURNED

AN EVENING SCENE ON THE SAME SUBJECT

Up! up! my Friend, and quit your books;
Or surely you'll grow double:
Up! up! my Friend, and clear your looks;
Why all this toil and trouble?

The sun, above the mountain's head,
A freshening lustre mellow
Through all the long green fields has spread,
His first sweet evening yellow.

Books! 'tis a dull and endless strife:
Come, hear the woodland linnet,
How sweet his music! on my life,
There's more of wisdom in it.

And hark! how blithe the throstle sings!
He, too, is no mean preacher:
Come forth into the light of things,
Let Nature be your Teacher.

She has a world of ready wealth,
Our minds and hearts to bless—
Spontaneous wisdom breathed by health,
Truth breathed by cheerfulness.

One impulse from a vernal wood
May teach you more of man,
Of moral evil and of good,
Than all the sages can.

Sweet is the lore which Nature brings;
Our meddling intellect
Mis-shapes the beauteous forms of things:–
We murder to dissect.

Enough of Science and of Art;
Close up those barren leaves;
Come forth, and bring with you a heart
That watches and receives.

THE SOLITARY REAPER

BEHOLD her, single in the field,
Yon solitary Highland Lass!
Reaping and singing by herself;
Stop here, or gently pass!
Alone she cuts and binds the grain,
And sings a melancholy strain;
O listen! for the Vale profound
Is overflowing with the sound.

No Nightingale did ever chaunt
More welcome notes to weary bands
Of travellers in some shady haunt,
Among Arabian sands:
A voice so thrilling ne'er was heard
In spring-time from the Cuckoo-bird,
Breaking the silence of the seas
Among the farthest Hebrides.

Will no one tell me what she sings?–
Perhaps the plaintive numbers flow
For old, unhappy, far-off things,
And battles long ago:
Or is it some more humble lay
Familiar matter of to-day?
Some natural sorrow, loss, or pain,
That has been, and may be again?

Whate'er the theme, the Maiden sang
As if her song could have no ending;
I saw her singing at her work,
And o'er the sickle bending;-
I listened, motionless and still;
And, as I mounted up the hill,
The music in my heart I bore,
Long after it was heard no more.

TINTERN ABBEY

Composed a few miles above Tintern Abbey, on revisiting the Banks of the Wye during a Tour. July 13, 1798

FIVE years have past; five summers, with the length
Of five long winters! and again I hear
These waters, rolling from their mountain-springs
With a soft inland murmur.–Once again
Do I behold these steep and lofty cliffs,
That on a wild secluded scene impress
Thoughts of more deep seclusion; and connect
The landscape with the quiet of the sky.
The day is come when I again repose
Here, under this dark sycamore, and view
These plots of cottage-ground, these orchard-tufts,
Which at this season, with their unripe fruits,
Are clad in one green hue, and lose themselves
'Mid groves and copses. Once again I see
These hedge-rows, hardly hedge-rows, little lines
Of sportive wood run wild: these pastoral farms,
Green to the very door; and wreaths of smoke
Sent up, in silence, from among the trees!
With some uncertain notice, as might seem
Of vagrant dwellers in the houseless woods,
Or of some Hermit's cave, where by his fire
The Hermit sits alone.

         These beauteous forms,
Through a long absence, have not been to me
As is a landscape to a blind man's eye:
But oft, in lonely rooms, and 'mid the din

Of towns and cities, I have owed to them,
In hours of weariness, sensations sweet,
Felt in the blood, and felt along the heart;
And passing even into my purer mind,
With tranquil restoration:–feelings too
Of unremembered pleasure: such, perhaps,
As have no slight or trivial influence
On that best portion of a good man's life,
His little, nameless, unremembered, acts
Of kindness and of love. Nor less, I trust,
To them I may have owed another gift,
Of aspect more sublime; that blessed mood,
In which the burthen of the mystery,
In which the heavy and the weary weight
Of all this unintelligible world,
Is lightened:–that serene and blessed mood,
In which the affections gently lead us on,–
Until, the breath of this corporeal frame
And even the motion of our human blood
Almost suspended, we are laid asleep
In body, and become a living soul:
While with an eye made quiet by the power
Of harmony, and the deep power of joy,
We see into the life of things.

                                          If this
Be but a vain belief, yet, oh! how oft–
In darkness and amid the many shapes
Of joyless daylight; when the fretful stir
Unprofitable, and the fever of the world,
Have hung upon the beatings of my heart–
How oft, in spirit, have I turned to thee,
O sylvan Wye! thou wanderer thro' the woods,
How often has my spirit turned to thee!
  And now, with gleams of half-extinguished thought,

With many recognitions dim and faint,
And somewhat of a sad perplexity,
The picture of the mind revives again:
While here I stand, not only with the sense
Of present pleasure, but with pleasing thoughts
That in this moment there is life and food
For future years. And so I dare to hope,
Though changed, no doubt, from what I was when first
I came among these hills; when like a roe
I bounded o'er the mountains, by the sides
Of the deep rivers, and the lonely streams,
Wherever nature led: more like a man
Flying from something that he dreads than one
Who sought the thing he loved. For nature then
(The coarser pleasures of my boyish days,
And their glad animal movements all gone by)
To me was all in all.—I cannot paint
What then I was. The sounding cataract
Haunted me like a passion: the tall rock,
The mountain, and the deep and gloomy wood,
Their colours and their forms, were then to me
An appetite: a feeling and a love,
That had no need of a remoter charm,
By thought supplied, nor any interest
Unborrowed from the eye.—That time is past,
And all its aching joys are now no more,
And all its dizzy raptures. Not for this
Faint I, nor mourn nor murmur: other gifts
Have followed: for such loss, I would believe,
Abundant recompense. For I have learned
To look on nature, not as in the hour
Of thoughtless youth; but hearing often-times
The still, sad music of humanity,
Nor harsh nor grating, though of ample power

To chasten and subdue. And I have felt
A presence that disturbs me with the joy
Of elevated thoughts; a sense sublime
Of something far more deeply interfused,
Whose dwelling is the light of setting suns,
And the round ocean and the living air,
And the blue sky, and in the mind of man:
A motion and a spirit, that impels
All thinking things, all objects of all thought,
And rolls through all things. Therefore am I still
A lover of the meadows and the woods,
And mountains; and of all that we behold
From this green earth; of all the mighty world
Of eye, and ear,—both what they half create,
And what perceive; well pleased to recognise
In nature and the language of the sense
The anchor of my purest thoughts, the nurse,
The guide, the guardian of my heart, and soul
Of all my moral being.
                              Nor perchance,
If I were not thus taught, should I the more
Suffer my genial spirits to decay:
For thou art with me here upon the banks
Of this fair river; thou my dearest Friend,
My dear, dear Friend; and in thy voice I catch
The language of my former heart, and read
My former pleasures in the shooting lights
Of thy wild eyes. Oh! yet a little while
May I behold in thee what I was once,
My dear, dear Sister! and this prayer I make,
Knowing that Nature never did betray
The heart that loved her; 'tis her privilege,
Through all the years of our life, to lead
From joy to joy: for she can so inform

ULLSWATER; SILVER BAY

The mind that is within us, so impress
With quietness and beauty, and so feed
With lofty thoughts, that neither evil tongues,
Rash judgements nor the sneers of selfish men,
Nor greetings where no kindness is, nor all
The dreary intercourse of daily life,
Shall e'er prevail against us, or disturb
Our cheerful faith, that all which we behold
Is full of blessings. Therefore let the moon
Shine on thee in thy solitary walk;
And let the misty mountain-winds be free
To blow against thee: and, in after years,
When these wild ecstasies shall be matured
Into a sober pleasure: when thy mind
Shall be a mansion for all lovely forms,
Thy memory be as a dwelling-place
For all sweet sounds and harmonies; oh! then,
If solitude, or fear, or pain, or grief,
Should be thy portion, with what healing thoughts
Of tender joy wilt thou remember me,
And these my exhortations! Nor, perchance–
If I should be where I no more can hear
Thy voice, nor catch from thy wild eyes these gleams
Of past existence–wilt thou then forget
That on the banks of this delightful stream
We stood together; and that I, so long
A worshipper of Nature, hither came
Unwearied in that service: rather say
With warmer love–oh! with far deeper zeal
Of holier love. Nor wilt thou then forget
That after many wanderings, many years
Of absence, these steep woods and lofty cliffs,
And this green pastoral landscape, were to me
More dear, both for themselves and for thy sake!

ALICE FELL

OR, POVERTY

THE post-boy drove with fierce career,
For threatening clouds the moon had drowned;
When, as we hurried on, my ear
Was smitten with a startling sound

As if the wind blew many ways,
I heard the sound,–and more and more;
It seemed to follow with the chaise,
And still I heard it as before.

At length I to the boy called out;
He stopped his horses at the word,
But neither cry, nor voice, nor shout,
Nor aught else like it, could be heard.

The boy then smacked his whip, and fast
The horses scampered through the rain;
But, hearing soon upon the blast
The cry, I bade him halt again.

Forthwith alighting on the ground,
'Whence comes,' said I, 'this piteous moan?'
And there a little Girl I found,
Sitting behind the chaise, alone.

'My cloak!' no other word she spake,
But loud and bitterly she wept,
As if her innocent heart would break;
And down from off her seat she leapt.

'What ails you, child?'–she sobbed, 'Look here!'
I saw it in the wheel entangled,
A weather-beaten rag as e'er
From any garden scare-crow dangled.

There, twisted between nave and spoke,
It hung, nor could at once be freed;
But our joint pains unloosed the cloak,
A miserable rag indeed!

'And whither are you going, child,
To-night along these lonesome ways?'
'To Durham,' answered she, half wild—
'Then come with me into the chaise.'

Insensible to all relief
Sat the poor girl, and forth did send
Sob after sob, as if her grief
Could never, never have an end.

'My child, in Durham do you dwell?'
She checked herself in her distress,
And said, 'My name is Alice Fell;
I'm fatherless and motherless.

'And I to Durham, Sir, belong.'
Again, as if the thought would choke
Her very heart, her grief grew strong;
And all was for her tattered cloak!

The chaise drove on; our journey's end
Was nigh; and sitting by my side,
As if she had lost her only friend
She wept, nor would be pacified.

Up to the tavern-door we post;
Of Alice and her grief I told;
And I gave money to the host,
To buy a new cloak for the old.

"And let it be of duffil grey,
As warm a cloak as man can sell!'
Proud creature was she the next day,
The little orphan, Alice Fell!

'TIS SAID THAT SOME HAVE DIED FOR LOVE

'Tis said that some have died for love:
And here and there a church-yard grave is found
In the cold north's unhallowed ground,
Because the wretched man himself had slain,
His love was such a grievous pain.
And there is one whom I five years have known;
He dwells alone
Upon Helvellyn's side:
He loved–the pretty Barbara died;
And thus he makes his moan:
Three years had Barbara in her grave been laid
When thus his moan he made:

'Oh, move, thou Cottage, from behind that oak!
Or let the aged tree uprooted lie,
That in some other way yon smoke
May mount into the sky!
The clouds pass on; they from the heavens depart;
I look–the sky is empty space;
I know not what I trace;
But when I cease to look, my hand is on my heart.

'O! what a weight is in these shades! Ye leaves,
That murmur once so dear, when will it cease?
Your sound my heart of rest bereaves,
It robs my heart of peace.
Thou Thrush, that singest loud–and loud and free,
Into yon row of willows flit,
Upon that alder sit;
Or sing another song, or choose another tree.

'Roll back, sweet Rill! back to thy mountain-bounds,
And there for ever be thy water chained!
For thou dost haunt the air with sounds
That cannot be sustained;
If still beneath that pine-tree's ragged bough
Headlong yon waterfall must come,
Oh let it then be dumb!
Be anything, sweet Rill, but that which thou art now.

'Thou Eglantine, so bright with sunny showers
Proud as a rainbow spanning half the vale,
Thou one fair shrub, oh! shed thy flowers,
And stir not in the gale.
For thus to see thee nodding in the air,
To see thy arch thus stretch and bend,
Thus rise and thus descend,–
Distrurbs me till the sight is more than I can bear.'

The Man who makes this feverish complaint
Is one of giant stature, who could dance
Equipped from head to foot in iron mail.
Ah gentle Love! if ever thought was thine
To store up kindred hours for me, thy face
Turn from me, gentle Love! nor let me walk
Within the sound of Emma's voice, nor know
Such happiness as I have known to-day.

SURPRISED BY JOY

SURPRISED by joy–impatient as the Wind
I turned to share the transport–Oh! with whom
But Thee, deep buried in the silent tomb,
That spot which no vicissitude can find?
Love, faithful love, recalled thee to my mind–
But how could I forget thee? Through what power,
Even for the least division of an hour,
Have I been so beguiled as to be blind
To my most grievous loss!–That thought's return
Was the worst pang that sorrow ever bore.
Save one, one only, when I stood forlorn,
Knowing my heart's best treasure was no more;
That neither present time, nor years unborn
Could to my sight that heavenly face restore.

MY HEART LEAPS UP

MY heart leaps up when I behold
        A rainbow in the sky:
So was it when my life began;
So is it now I am a man;
So be it when I shall grow old,
        Or let me die!
The Child is father of the Man;
And I could wish my days to be
Bound each to each by natural piety.

ODE

Extracts from Immortality Ode

I

THERE was a time when meadow, grove, and stream,
The earth, and every common sight,
　　　To me did seem
　　Apparelled in celestial light,
The glory and the freshness of a dream.
It is not now as it hath been of yore;–
　　Turn wheresoe'er I may,
　　　By night or day,
The things which I have seen I now can see no more.

II

　　The Rainbow comes and goes,
　　And lovely is the Rose,
　　The Moon doth with delight
Look round her when the heavens are bare,
　　Waters on a starry night
　　Are beautiful and fair;
　The sunshine is a glorious birth;
　But yet I know, where'er I go,
That there hath past away a glory from the earth.

A SLUMBER DID MY SPIRIT SEAL

A SLUMBER did my spirit seal;
　I had no human fears:
She seemed a thing that could not feel
　The touch of early years.

No motion has she now, no force;
　She neither hears nor sees;
Rolled round in earth's diurnal course,
　With rocks, and stones and trees.

WE ARE SEVEN

—A Simple Child,
That lightly draws its breath,
And feels its life in every limb,
What should it know of death?

I met a little cottage Girl:
She was eight years old, she said;
Her hair was thick with many a curl
That clustered round her head.

She had a rustic, woodland air,
And she was wildly clad:
Her eyes were fair, and very fair;
–Her beauty made me glad.

'Sisters and brothers, little maid
How many may you be?'
'How many? Seven in all,' she said,
And wondering looked at me.

'And where are they? I pray you tell.'
She answered, 'Seven are we;
And two of us at Conway dwell,
And two are gone to sea.

'Two of us in the church-yard lie,
My sister and my brother;
And, in the church-yard cottage, I
Dwell near them with my mother.'

'You say that two at Conway dwell,
And two are gone to sea,
Yet ye are seven! I pray you tell,
Sweet Maid, how this may be.'

Then did the little Maid reply,
'Seven boys and girls are we;
Two of us in the church-yard lie,
Beneath the church-yard tree.'

'You run about, my little Maid,
Your limbs they are alive;
If two are in the church-yard laid,
Then ye are only five.'

'Their graves are green, they may be seen,'
The little Maid replied,
'Twelve steps or more from my mother's door,
And they are side by side.

'My stockings there I often knit,
My kerchief there I hem;
And there upon the ground I sit,
And sing a song to them.

'And often after sun-set Sir,
When it is light and fair,
I take my little porringer,
And eat my supper there.

'The first that died was sister Jane:
In bed she moaning lay,
Till God released her of her pain;
And then she went away.

'So in the church-yard, she was laid;
And, when the grass was dry,
Together round her grave we played,
My brother John and I.

'And when the ground was white with snow,
And I could run and slide,
My brother John was forced to go,
And he lies by her side.'

'How many are you, then,' said I,
'If they two are in heaven?'
Quick was the little Maid's reply,
O Master! we are seven.'

'But they are dead; those two are dead!
Their spirits are in heaven!'
'Twas throwing words away; for still
The little maid would have her will,
And said, 'Nay, we are seven!'

WILLIAM WORDSWORTH

BEGGARS

SHE had a tall man's height or more;
Her face from summer's noontide heat
No bonnet shaded, but she wore,
A mantle, to her very feet
Descending with a graceful flow,
And on her head a cap as white as new-fallen snow.

Her skin was of Egyptian brown:
Haughty, as if her eye had seen
Its own light to a distance thrown,
She towered, fit person for a Queen
To lead those ancient Amazonian files;
Or ruling Bandit's wife among the Grecian isles.

Advancing, forth she stretched her hand
And begged an alms with doleful plea
That ceased not; on our English land
Such woes, I knew, could never be;
And yet a boon I gave her, for the creature
Was beautiful to see–a weed of glorious feature.

I left her, and pursued my way;
And soon before me did espy
A pair of little Boys at play,
Chasing a crimson butterfly;
The taller followed with his hat in hand,
Wreathed round with yellow flowers the gayest of the land.

The other wore a rimless crown
With leaves of laurel stuck about;
And while both followed up and down,
Each whooping with a merry shout,
In their fraternal features I could trace
Unquestionable lines of that wild Suppliant's face.

Yet *they*, so blithe of heart, seemed fit
For finest tasks of earth or air:
Wings let them have, and they might flit
Precursors to Aurora's car,
Scattering fresh flowers: though happier far, I ween,
To hunt their fluttering game o'er rock and level green.

They dart across my path–but lo,
Each ready with a plaintive whine!
Said I, 'not half an hour ago
Your Mother has had alms of mine.'
'That cannot be,' one answered–'she is dead:'
I looked reproof–they saw–but neither hung his head.

'She has been dead, Sir, many a day.'-
'Hush, boys! you're telling me a lie;
It was your Mother, as I say!'
And in the twinkling of an eye,
'Come! come!' cried one, and without more ado
Off to some other play the joyous Vagrants flew!

THE COMPLAINT

OF A FORSAKEN INDIAN WOMAN

I

BEFORE I see another day,
Oh let my body die away!
In sleep I heard the northern gleams;
The stars, they were among my dreams;
In rustling conflict through the skies,
I heard, I saw the flashes drive,
And yet they are upon my eyes,
And yet I am alive;
Before I see another day,
Oh let my body die away!

II

My fire is dead: it knew no pain;
Yet is it dead, and I remain:
All stiff with ice the ashes lie;
And they are dead, and I will die.
When I was well, I wished to live,
For clothes, for warmth, for food, and fire;
But they to me no joy can give,
No pleasure now, and no desire.
Then here contented will I lie!
Alone, I cannot fear to die.

III

Alas! ye might have dragged me on
Another day, a single one!
Too soon I yielded to despair;
Why did ye listen to my prayer?
When ye were gone my limbs were stronger;
And oh, how greviously I rue,
That, afterwards, a little longer,
My friends, I did not follow you!
For strong and without pain I lay,
Dear friends, when ye were gone away.

IV

My Child! they gave thee to another,
A woman who was not thy mother.
When from my arms my Babe they took,
On me how strangely did he look!
Through his whole body something ran,
A most strange working did I see;
—As if he strove to be a man,
That he might pull the sledge for me:
And then he stretched his arms, how wild!
Oh mercy! like a helpless child.

V

My little joy! my little pride!
In two days more I must have died.
Then do not weep and grieve for me;
I feel I must have died with thee.
O wind, that oe-er my head art flying
The way my friends their course did bend,
I should not feel the pain of dying,
Could I with thee a message send;
Too soon, my friends, ye went away;
For I had many things to say.

VI

I'll follow you across the snow;
Ye travel heavily and slow;
In spite of all my weary pain
I'll look upon your tents again.
—My fire is dead, and snowy white
The water which beside it stood:
The wolf has come to me to-night,
And he has stolen away my food.
For ever left alone am I;
Then wherefore should I fear to die?

VII

Young as I am, my course is run,
I shall not see another sun;
I cannot lift my limbs to know
If they have any life or no.
My poor forsaken Child, if I
For once could have thee close to me,
With happy heart I then would die,
And my last thought would happy be;
But thou, dear Babe, art far away,
Nor shall I see another day.

UPON WESMINSTER BRIDGE
COMPOSED SEPTEMBER 3, 1802

EARTH has not anything to show more fair:
Dull would he be of soul who could pass by
A sight so touching in its majesty:
This City now doth, like a garment, wear
The beauty of the morning; silent, bare,
Ships, towers, domes, theatres, and temples lie
Open unto the fields, and to the sky;
All bright and glittering in the smokeless air.
Never did sun more beautifully steep
In his first splendour, valley, rock, or hill:
Ne'er saw I, never felt, a calm, so deep!
The river glideth at his own sweet will:
Dear God! the very houses seem asleep;
And all that mighty heart is lying still!

THE AFFLICTION OF MARGARET

I

WHERE art thou, my beloved Son.
Where are thou, worse to me than dead?
Oh find me. prosperous or undone!
Or, if the grave be now thy bed,
Why am I ignorant of the same,
That I may rest: and neither blame
Nor sorrow may attend thy name?

II

Seven years, alas! to have received
No tidings of an only child;
To have despaired, have hoped, believed,
And been for evermore beguiled;
Sometimes with thoughts of very bliss!
I catch at them, and then I miss;
Was ever darkness like to this?

III

He was among the prime in worth,
An object beauteous to behold;
Well born, well bred; I sent him forth
Ingenuous, innocent, and bold:
If things ensued that wanted grace,
As hath been said, they were not base;
And never blush was on my face.

IV

Ah! little doth the young-one dream,
When full of play and childish cares,
What power is in his wildest scream,
Heard by his mother unawares!
He knows it not, he cannot guess:
Years to a mother bring distress;
But do not make her love the less.

V

Neglect me! no, I suffered long,
From that ill thought; and, being blind,
Said, 'Pride shall help me in my wrong:
Kind mother have I been, as kind
As ever breathed:' and that is true;
I've wet my path with tears like dew,
Weeping for him when no one knew.

VI

My Son, if thou be humbled, poor,
hopeless of honour and of gain,
Oh! do not dread thy mother's door:
Think not of me with grief and pain:
I now can see with better eyes;
And worldly grandeur I despise,
And fortune with her gifts and lies.

VII

Alas! the fowls of heaven have wings,
And blasts of heaven will aid their flight:
They mount–how short a voyage brings
The wanderers back to their delight!
Chains tie us down by land and sea;
And wishes, vain as mine, may be
All that is left to comfort thee.

VIII

Perhaps some dungeon hears thee groan,
Maimed, mangled by inhuman men;
Or thou upon a desert thrown
Inheritest the lion's den;
Or hast been summoned to the deep,
Thou, thou and all thy mates, to keep
An incommunicable sleep.

IX

I look for ghosts; but none will force
Their way to me: 'tis falsely said
That there was ever intercourse
Between the living and the dead;
For, surely, then I should have sight
Of him I wait for day and night,
With love and longings infinite.

Word Problems

JAMESTOWN'S

Number Power

Kenneth Tamarkin

JAMESTOWN PUBLISHERS

a division of NTC/CONTEMPORARY PUBLISHING GROUP

Lincolnwood, Illinois USA

ISBN: 0-8092-2278-7

Published by Jamestown Publishers,
a division of NTC/Contemporary Publishing Group, Inc.,
4255 West Touhy Avenue,
Lincolnwood (Chicago), Illinois 60712-1975 U.S.A.

2 3 4 5 6 7 8 9 10 11 12 021 10 09 08 07 06

Table of Contents

Multiplication and Division Word Problems: Whole Numbers

Multiplication and Division Word Problems: Decimals and Fractions

Using Proportions

To the Student

Welcome to *Word Problems*.

This workbook is designed to help you understand how to solve word problems found in the workplace and in your everyday experiences. The first section of the book, Building Number Power, provides step-by-step instruction and practice in reading and solving word problems. The last section of the book, Using Number Power, provides further practice in solving word problems in real-life situations.

Throughout this book, you will be encouraged to use mental math. You will see word problems with small or easy to compute numbers. Once you figure out which math operation you should use, you might be able to do the math in your head.

Also scattered through the book are tips on estimation and using a calculator. The following icons will alert you to the problems where using these skills will be especially helpful.

 calculation icon

 estimation icon

 mental math icon

To get the most from your work, do each problem carefully. Inside the back cover is a chart to help you keep track of your score on each exercise.

Also included in the back of the book are quick reference pages for using a calculator, estimation, mental math, and formulas and measurements. Refer to these pages for a quick review and helpful explanation.

Word Problem Pretest

This test will tell you which sections of *Word Problems* you need to concentrate on. Do every problem that you can. Round decimals to the nearest cent or the nearest hundredth. After you check your answers, the chart at the end of the test will guide you to the pages of the book where you need work.

1. 1,600 pounds of steel are used to make a Chevrolet. The automobile plant produced 840 Chevrolets in one day. How many pounds of steel were needed that day to make the cars?

    a. 2,440 pounds
    b. 1,344,000 pounds
    c. 760 pounds
    d. 244,000 pounds
    e. none of the above

2. In one year, Melinda grew $2\frac{1}{4}$ inches to $48\frac{3}{8}$ inches. What was her height at the beginning of the year?

    a. $50\frac{5}{8}$ inches

    b. $46\frac{1}{8}$ inches

    c. $43\frac{1}{2}$ inches

    d. $21\frac{1}{2}$ inches

    e. $108\frac{27}{32}$ inches

3. Cynthia took 19 girls roller blading. If it cost $0.75 for each of the children to get in and $0.50 for each of them to rent roller blades, how much money did Cynthia have to collect?

    a. $20.25
    b. $23.75
    c. $17.75
    d. $1.25
    e. $4.75

4. During the big spring sale, Jean bought a coat for $79.50, which was 75% of the original price. What was the original price of the coat?

    a. $106.00
    b. $59.63
    c. $154.50
    d. $94.34
    e. not enough information given

5. Diana makes lemonade from the powdered concentrate by combining 5 tablespoons of concentrate with 2 cups of water. The directions say you should use 24 cups of water for the entire container of concentrate. How many tablespoons of concentrate are in the container?

   a. 240 tablespoons
   b. 130 tablespoons
   c. 110 tablespoons
   d. 60 tablespoons
   e. 31 tablespoons

6. Carol was told that she would have to pay $684 interest on a $3,600 loan. What interest rate would she have to pay?

   a. $2,912
   b. $4,284
   c. 19%
   d. 5.3%
   e. 81%

7. Jack bought a turkey for $10.34 and a chicken for $5.17. How much did he spend on the meat?

   a. $2.00
   b. $5.17
   c. $15.51
   d. $53.46
   e. $20.00

8. The New Software Company received a shipment of 200,000 foam pellets to be used in packing boxes. If New Software uses on the average 400 pellets for each box, how many boxes can be packed using the shipment of pellets?

   a. 2,000 boxes
   b. 800 boxes
   c. 199,600 boxes
   d. 80,000,000 boxes
   e. 500 boxes

9. Oranges cost $2.40 a dozen. Winsome bought the fruit pictured here. How much money did she spend on the oranges?

   a. $7.20
   b. $2.44
   c. $2.36
   d. $0.80
   e. $0.60

10. A roast weighing 3.15 pounds is cut into 24 slices. On the average, how much does each slice weigh?

    a. 27.15 pounds
    b. 20.85 pounds
    c. 75.60 pounds
    d. 0.13 pounds
    e. 1.31 pounds

11. Barbara needed 180 inches of masking tape to mask a window for painting. How many rolls of masking tape does she need to mask 12 of these identical windows?

    a. 18 feet
    b. 15 rolls
    c. 192 inches
    d. 168 inches
    e. not enough information given

12. A factory produces $\frac{7}{8}$-ton steel girders. How much steel does the factory need to produce 600 of the girders?

    a. 525 tons
    b. 52.5 tons
    c. 686 tons
    d. 68.6 tons
    e. none of the above

13. During the sale, Naisuon bought a three-piece wool suit that was reduced by $98 to $190. What was the original price of the suit?

    a. $92
    b. $288
    c. $276
    d. $96
    e. $291

14. Out of 1,400 people polled, 68% were in favor of a nuclear arms freeze, 25% were against it, and the rest were undecided. How many people were undecided?

    a. 93 people
    b. 350 people
    c. 952 people
    d. 98 people
    e. 1,307 people

15. A $1\frac{1}{4}$-pound lobster costs \$7.80. How much does it cost per pound?

    a. \$9.75
    b. \$6.24
    c. \$6.55
    d. \$9.05
    e. \$1.56

16. At the gas station, Verna tried to fill up her 18-gallon gas tank. When the tank was filled, the gasoline pump looked like the picture at right. How much gas was in the tank before Verna started pumping the gas?

    a. 0.71 gallon
    b. 71 gallons
    c. 5.22 gallons
    d. 6.78 gallons
    e. 30.78 gallons

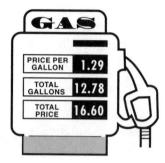

17. During the Washington's birthday clearance sale, Gayle bought a \$96 coat that was reduced by $\frac{1}{3}$. What was the sale price of the coat?

    a. \$32
    b. \$64
    c. \$288
    d. \$93
    e. none of the above

18. Shorie's rent has been increased \$65 a month to \$780 a month. What had she been paying?

    a. \$715
    b. \$845
    c. \$72
    d. \$9,360
    e. \$50,700

19. Lillian's allergy pills come in the bottle pictured at the right. She takes four tablets a day. How many tablets did she have left after taking the tablets for 30 days?

    a. 130 tablets
    b. 216 tablets
    c. 120 tablets
    d. 370 tablets
    e. not enough information given

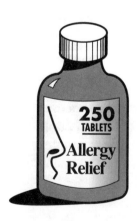

20. A cereal manufacturer puts 2 ounces of sugar in every box of cereal. How many pounds of sugar are needed for 1,000 boxes?

  a. 50 pounds
  b. 20 pounds
  c. 125 pounds
  d. 200 pounds
  e. 625 pounds

21. For the survey to be considered valid, 15% of the 6,000 questionnaires had to be returned. At least how many questionnaires had to be returned?

  a. 900 questionnaires
  b. 400 questionnaires
  c. 40,000 questionnaires
  d. 5,985 questionnaires
  e. not enough information given

22. An oil truck carried 9,008 gallons of oil. After making seven deliveries averaging 364 gallons each, how much oil was left in the truck?

  a. 174 gallons
  b. 9,379 gallons
  c. 8,644 gallons
  d. 6,460 gallons
  e. 8,637 gallons

23. In one week, Speculation Company's stock dropped in value $1\frac{7}{8}$ dollars to $8\frac{3}{4}$ dollars a share. What was the value of the stock at the beginning of the week?

  a. $2\frac{4}{5}$ dollars
  b. $16\frac{13}{32}$ dollars
  c. $6\frac{7}{8}$ dollars
  d. $10\frac{5}{8}$ dollars
  e. $9\frac{5}{6}$ dollars

24. How much would a 1.62-pound package of lamb shoulder chops cost at $2.43 a pound?

  a. $1.50
  b. $4.05
  c. $0.81
  d. $15.00
  e. $3.94

25. Money available for financial aid at Santa Carla Community College has dropped $462,000 from last year's $1,126,200. The college decided to divide the aid equally among 820 students who needed the money. How much did each student get in financial aid?

    a. $563.41
    b. $810.00
    c. $1,373.41
    d. $1,936.82
    e. none of the above

Questions 26–28 are based on the following information:

The Bargain Basement marks down clothes depending on how long they have been displayed. The day an item is put on the racks or in a bin, a date ticket and a price tag are attached to it. The chart shows the amount of discount if the date ticket is at least the listed number of days old.

Days	Markdown
10 days	10%
20 days	25%
30 days	40%
40 days	75%

26. On May 30, Sharon went shopping at the Bargain Basement. She found one blouse she wanted dated April 14 with a price tag of $18. How much did she have to pay for the blouse?

    a. 46 days
    b. $13.40
    c. $4.50
    d. $22.50
    e. $18.00

27. On July 20 at the Bargain Basement, Belquis selected five bathing suits. The red bathing suit was dated June 28 and had a $40 price tag. The floral print suit was dated July 8 and had a price tag of $30. The violet bathing suit was dated June 18 and had a price of $45. The striped bathing suit was dated July 15 and had a price of $28. The black bathing suit was dated June 2 and had a price of $60. Which bathing suit was the least expensive?

    a. the red bathing suit
    b. the floral print bathing suit
    c. the violet bathing suit
    d. the striped bathing suit
    e. the black bathing suit

28. On December 3 at the Bargain Basement in New Hampshire, Marcia bought a sweater dated November 28. She paid with a $50 bill. Since New Hampshire does not have a sales tax, she paid no tax. How much change did Marcia receive?

   a. $11.00
   b. $89.00
   c. $19.50
   d. $14.90
   e. not enough information given

29. Last month, Francisco used 445 kWh of electricity in his home. On his bill, there was a customer charge of $5.81, a delivery service charge of $0.047 per kWh, and a supplier service charge of $0.032 per kWh. Which expression could be used to calculate his total bill?

   a. 445 kWh ($5.81 + $0.047 + $0.032)
   b. $5.81 + $0.047 + $0.032
   c. $5.81 + 445 kWh ($0.047 + $0.032)
   d. 445 kWh + $5.81 ($0.047 + $0.032)
   e. 445 kWh ($0.047 + $0.032)

30. Brunilda was trying to decide between buying a digital camera and a single lens reflex (SLR) camera. The digital camera cost $499 while the SLR camera cost $249. Film for the SLR camera costs $4 for a roll of 36 pictures, plus $16 for developing. Digital pictures can be stored on a Zip disk, which costs $10 and holds 720 pictures. How many pictures would Brunilda have to take for the cost of each camera plus the pictures to be the same?

   a. 13 pictures
   b. 250 pictures
   c. 260 pictures
   d. 468 pictures
   e. 756 pictures

Word Problem Pretest Chart

If you miss more than one problem in any section of this test, you should complete the lessons on the practice pages indicated on this chart. If you miss no problems in a section of this test, you may not need further study in this chapter. However, to master solving word problems, we recommend that you work through the entire book. As you do, focus on the skills covered in each chapter.

PROBLEM NUMBERS	SKILL AREA	PRACTICE PAGES
13, 18	add or subtract whole numbers	18–39
1, 8	multiply or divide whole numbers	61–76
2, 23	add or subtract fractions	52–60
12, 15	multiply or divide fractions	80–88
7, 16	add or subtract decimals	40–51, 56–60
10, 24	multiply or divide decimals	77–79, 87–88
4, 6, 21	percents	118–136
9, 20	conversion	100–101
11, 28	not enough information	110–114
3, 5, 14, 17, 19, 22, 25, 26, 27, 29, 30	multistep word problems	137–161

Building
Number
Power

INTRODUCTION TO WORD PROBLEMS

Steps in Solving Word Problems

A **word problem** is a sentence or group of sentences that tells a story, contains numbers, and asks the reader to find another number.

This is an example of a word problem:

Last week Paula earned $194. The week before, she earned $288. What was the total amount of money she earned?

In this book, you will use five steps to solve word problems. It is important to follow these steps to organize your thinking. They will help you figure out what may seem to be a difficult puzzle. In all cases, read the problem carefully, more than once if necessary. Then follow these steps.

STEP 1 Decide what the *question* is asking you to find.

STEP 2 Then, decide what *information* is *necessary* in order to solve the problem.

STEP 3 Next, decide what *arithmetic operation* to use.

STEP 4 Work out the problem and find the solution. Check your arithmetic.

STEP 5 Finally, *reread the question* to make sure that your answer *is sensible*.

Many people can do some word problems in their heads. This is known as **math intuition** and works well with small whole numbers. Math intuition often breaks down with larger numbers, decimals, and especially fractions. Additionally, word problems of two or more steps can be even more difficult.

You should practice the five-step approach even with problems that you could solve in your head. Then you will have something to fall back on when intuition is not enough.

Step 1: The Question

After reading a word problem, the first step in solving it is to decide what is being asked for. You must find the question.

The following word problem consists of only one sentence. This sentence asks a question and contains the information that is needed to solve the problem.

EXAMPLE 1   How much did Mel spend on dinner when the food cost $20 and the tax was $1?

The question asks, "How much did Mel spend on dinner?"

The next word problem contains two sentences. One sentence asks the question, and the other sentence gives the information that is necessary to solve the problem.

EXAMPLE 2   Mary got $167 a month in food stamps for 9 months. What was the total value of the stamps?

The question asks, "What was the total value of the stamps?"

Example 3 also contains two sentences. Notice that *both* sentences contain information that is necessary to solve the problem.

EXAMPLE 3   The Little Sweetheart tea set normally costs $8.95. How much did Alice save by buying the tea set for her daughter at an after-Christmas sale for $5.49?

The question asks, "How much did Alice save?"

Sometimes the question does not have a question mark.

EXAMPLE 4   Fredi has $27 in her checking account. She wrote checks for $15 and $20. Find how much money she needs to deposit in order to cover the checks.

The question asks, "Find how much money she needs to deposit in order to cover the checks."

Underline the question in each of the following word problems. DO NOT SOLVE!

1. Last winter it snowed 5 inches in December, 17 inches in January, 13 inches in February, and 2 inches in March. How much snow fell during the entire winter?

2. To cook the chicken, first brown it for 10 minutes. Then lower the temperature and let it simmer for 20 more minutes. What is the total cooking time?

3. Find the cost of parking at the meter for 3 hours if it costs 25 cents an hour to park.

4. How many years did Joe serve in prison if his sentence of five years was reduced by three for good behavior?

5. Jenny loves to plant flowers. She has $30 to spend on flower plant flats. Find the number of flats she can buy if they cost $4.98 each.

6. The recycling plant pays $22 a ton for recycled newspaper. How much did the city of Eugene receive when it delivered 174 tons of newspaper to the recycling plant?

In each of the following word problems, the question is missing. Write a possible question for each word problem.

7. A factory needs $2\frac{1}{3}$ yards of material to make a coat. The material comes in 60-yard rolls.

8. A tablet of Extra-Strength Tylenol contains 500 milligrams of acetaminophen. The normal adult dose is 2 tablets every 4 to 6 hours, not to exceed 8 tablets in 24 hours.

9. Computer Connection slashed the price of its best selling digital camera from $799 to $549.

10. The Arctictec textile factory, which operates round the clock, can produce 42,000 yards of Arctictec fabric in a 24-hour day.

11. In a normal week, Great Deal Used Cars sells 38 cars. During the big Presidents' Week sale, Great Deal sold 114 cars.

12. The snack bar menu, shown at the right, was posted on the wall.

Super Pretzels	$1.50
Chips	$.65
Nachos	$2.25
Soda (12 oz can)	$.80
Hot Dog	$2.00
Hamburger	$2.50
Pizza Slice	$1.75
Milk	$.75

Step 2: Selecting the Necessary Information

After finding the question, the next step in solving a word problem is selecting the **necessary information.** The necessary information consists of the **numbers** and the **labels** (words or symbols) that go with the numbers. The necessary information includes *only* the numbers and labels that you need to solve the problem.

The labels make the numbers in word problems concrete. For example, the necessary information in Example 1 below is not just the number 5, but includes *5 apples.* Paying close attention to labels will help you learn many of the methods shown in this book and will help you avoid common mistakes with word problems.

After each of the following examples, the necessary information is listed.

EXAMPLE 1   Doreen bought 5 apples last week and 6 apples this week. How many apples did she buy altogether?

The necessary information is *5 apples* and *6 apples.* Both numbers are followed by the label word *apples.*

EXAMPLE 2   A shirt costs $9.99. What is the cost of 5 shirts?

The necessary information is *$9.99* and *5 shirts.* The labels are the dollar sign (*$*) and the word *shirts.*

EXAMPLE 3   Four ounces of detergent are needed to clean a load of laundry. How many more loads of laundry can you clean if you buy the large bottle of detergent rather than the small bottle shown at right?

The necessary information is *4 ounces, 64 ounces,* and *96 ounces.* The numbers are followed by the label word *ounces.* Note that you get some of the necessary information from the pictures.

64 ounces   96 ounces

In each word problem, find the necessary information. Circle the numbers and underline the labels. Then write the label that would be a part of the answer, but DO NOT SOLVE!

1. On Friday a commuter train took 124 commuters to work and 119 commuters home. How many commuters rode the train that day?

2. There are 14 potatoes in the bag at the right. What is the average weight of each potato?

3. Unleaded gasoline costs $0.06 more per gallon than regular. Regular costs $1.47 a gallon. How much does unleaded gasoline cost?

4. To make the punch, Lona combined the bottle of ginger ale with the container of fruit juice shown at the right. How much punch did she make?

5. The radio station added $38 more to the $329 already in the superjackpot. What is the new amount of money in the superjackpot?

6. Frank bought the package of loose-leaf paper shown at the right and put 60 pages in his binder. How many pages were left in the package?

Necessary vs. Given Information

Sometimes a word problem contains numbers that aren't needed to answer the question. You must read problems carefully to choose only the necessary information.

Notice this important difference: The **given information** includes *all* of the numbers and labels in a word problem.

The **necessary information** includes *only* those numbers and labels needed to solve the problem.

EXAMPLE 1 Nelson travels to and from work with 3 friends every day. The round trip is 9 miles. If he works 5 days a week, how many miles does he commute in a week?

given information: 3 friends, 9 miles, 5 days
necessary information: 9 miles, 5 days

To figure out how many miles he commutes in a week, you do not need to know that Nelson travels with 3 friends.

EXAMPLE 2 There are 7,000 people living in Dry Gulch. Of the 3,000 people who are registered to vote, only 1,700 people participated in the last election. How many registered voters did not vote?

given information: 7,000 people, 3,000 people, 1,700 people
necessary information: 3,000 people, 1,700 people

All of the numbers have the same label—*people*. However, the total number of people in the town (7,000) is not needed.

Sometimes you will have to choose necessary information from a chart or picture containing other information as well.

EXAMPLE 3 According to the chart, how many hours did Eduardo work on Friday and Saturday?

given information: 4 hours, 2 hours, 6 hours, 8 hours
necessary information: 6 hours, 8 hours

Hours Worked	
Monday	4
Wednesday	2
Friday	6
Saturday	8

In this book, you will practice choosing information from charts and pictures.

This exercise will help you tell the difference between given and necessary information. Underline the given information. Circle the necessary information. DO NOT SOLVE!

1. Mona is 22 years old. She has a sister who is 20 years old and a boyfriend who is 23. How much older is Mona than her sister.

2. Rena receives $186 a month from welfare. She also receives $167 a month in food stamps in order to help feed her two children. How much public assistance does she receive each month?

3. Marilyn works three times as many hours as her 20-year-old sister Laura. Laura works 10 hours a week. How many hours a week does Marilyn work?

4. Suzanne has a 7-year-old car. According to the chart at the right, how much did she spend on gasoline during the first 2 months of the year?

Gasoline Expenses	
January	$43
February	$39
March	$40
April	$31

5. During the winter, the Right Foot shoe store spent $2,460 for oil heat and sold $35,800 worth of shoes. If oil costs $1.20 per gallon, how many gallons did the shoe store buy?

6. Erma, who is 45 years old, cooks dinner for the eight people in her family. Her husband, Jack, cooks breakfast in the morning for only half of the family. For how many people does Jack cook?

7. In a factory of 4,700 workers, 3,900 are skilled laborers. Of the employees, 700 people are on layoff. How many people are currently working?

8. Maritza bought the bottle of cola shown at the right for $1.49. How many 12-ounce glasses can she fill from the bottle?

Cola

64 OZ

ADDITION AND SUBTRACTION WORD PROBLEMS: WHOLE NUMBERS

Finding Addition Key Words

In the first chapter, you worked on finding the question and the necessary information in a word problem. The third step in solving a word problem is **deciding which arithmetic operation to use.**

You will now look at word problems that can be solved by using either addition or subtraction. In this book, you will learn five methods to decide whether to add or subtract.

> **1.** finding the key words
> **2.** restating the problem
> **3.** making drawings and diagrams
> **4.** writing number sentences
> **5.** using algebra

You will also work with making estimates and substitutions.

All of these methods are useful in understanding and solving word problems. After learning them, you may decide to use one or more of the methods that you find most helpful.

How do you know that you must add to solve a word problem? **Key words** can be helpful. A key word is a clue that can help you decide which arithmetic operation to use.

> **Note:** *How many, how much,* and *what* are general mathematics question words, but they are not key words. They help to identify the question but do not tell you whether to add, subtract, multiply, or divide.

The following examples contain addition key words.

EXAMPLE 1   What is the sum of 3 dollars and 2 dollars?

addition key words: sum, and

The sum is the answer to an addition problem. Therefore, when the word *sum* appears in a word problem, it is a clue that you should probably add to solve the problem.

EXAMPLE 2   The small cup contains 16 ounces of soda. The large cup contains 6 more ounces. How many ounces are in the large cup?

addition key word: more

The word *more* suggests that you should add the two amounts together.

....

**In the following exercise, circle the key words that suggest addition.
DO NOT SOLVE!**

1. Karen bought a new car for $15,640 plus $4,600 for options. How much did she spend for the car?

2. Judy bought four lemons and twelve oranges. How many pieces of fruit did she buy altogether?

3. A recipe for pumpkin pie says that an extra 2 tablespoons of sugar can be added to extra sweetness. The standard recipe is below. How many tablespoons of sugar are needed for the sweeter pie?

4. The price of a $6 general admission ticket to the ballpark will increase $1 next year. What will be the general admission price next year?

> **GRANNY'S PUMPKIN PIE**
> 1 tsp salt
> 4 tablespoons sugar
> 2 tsp. cinnamon

6. When Nancy did her kid's laundry, she found the coins pictured below. How much change did she find in all?

5. Although she has lost 15 pounds, Pam wants to lose 10 more. How much weight does she want to lose altogether?

Solving Addition Word Problems with Key Words

You have now looked at the first three steps in solving a word problem.

> **STEP 1**   Finding the question
> **STEP 2**   Selecting the necessary information
> **STEP 3**   Deciding what arithmetic operation to use

The next step in solving a word problem is doing the arithmetic. People who have not learned to think carefully about word problems may rush into doing the arithmetic and become confused. However, the three steps before doing the arithmetic and the one step after provide a good way to organize your thinking to solve a problem. The actual arithmetic is only one of several necessary steps.

Sometimes the arithmetic can be done in your head as **mental math.** Here are some examples that can be done as mental math.

EXAMPLE 1   What is the sum of 3 dollars and 2 dollars?

> **STEP 1**   *question:* What is the sum?
>
> **STEP 2**   *necessary information:* 3 dollars, 2 dollars
>
> **STEP 3**   *addition key words:* sum, and
>
> **STEP 4**   *add:* 3 dollars + 2 dollars = **5 dollars**

$$\begin{array}{r} 3 \\ + 2 \\ \hline 5 \end{array}$$

EXAMPLE 2   The small cup contains 16 ounces of soda. The large cup contains 6 more ounces. How many ounces are in the large cup?

> **STEP 1**   *question:* How many ounces are in the large cup?
>
> **STEP 2**   *necessary information:* 16 ounces, 6 ounces
>
> **STEP 3**   *addition key word:* more
>
> **STEP 4**   *add:* 16 ounces + 6 ounces = **22 ounces**

$$\begin{array}{r} 16 \\ + 6 \\ \hline 22 \end{array}$$

Once you have completed the arithmetic, there is one last step: reread the question and make sure that the answer is sensible.

For instance, if you had subtracted in Example 2, you would have gotten an answer of 10 ounces. Would it have made sense to say that the smaller cup was 16 ounces and the larger cup was 10 ounces?

**For each problem, circle the key word or words and do the arithmetic.
Be sure to include the label as part of your answer.**

1. After 5 inches of snow fell on a base of 23 inches of snow, how
   many inches of snow were on the ski trail altogether?

2. According to the chart at the right, what was the new bus fare
   to Georgetown after the 1999 fare was increased by 20 cents?

Bus Fares 1999	
Holliston	$.85
Green Borough	$1.75
Georgetown	$1.80
Filmore	$2.60

3. What is the total weight of a 3,500-pound truck carrying a
   720-pound load?

4. How big an apartment is the Dao family looking for if they want
   one that is 2 rooms larger than their 3-room apartment?

5. After the church raised $121,460 the first year and $89,742 the
   second, how much money was in its building fund?

6. According to the price chart at the right, how much does it cost
   to buy both a sofa and a reclining chair?

Furniture	
Sofa	$529
Love seat	$319
Reclining chair	$449
Coffee table	$199

Finding Subtraction Key Words

Each of the key words in the previous exercises helped you decide to add. Other key words may help you decide to subtract. Here is an example of a word problem using subtraction key words.

EXAMPLE   The large cup contains 16 ounces of soda. The small cup contains 6 ounces less than the large cup. How many ounces does the small cup contain?

> **STEP 1**   *question:* How many ounces does the small cup contain?
>
> **STEP 2**   *necessary information:* 16 ounces, 6 ounces
>
> **STEP 3**   *subtraction key words:* less than

> **Note:** In some subtraction word problems, the key words *less* and *than* are separated by other words. This is also true for *more* and *than*.

In the following exercise, circle the key words that suggest subtraction. DO NOT SOLVE!

1. Bargain Airlines is $25 cheaper than First Class Air. First Class charges $200 for a flight from Kansas City to St. Louis. What does Bargain Airlines charge?

2. Out of 7,103 students, State College had 1,423 graduates last year. This year there were 1,251 graduates. What was the decrease in the number of graduates?

3. The small steak weighs 5 ounces less than the large steak. How much does the small steak weigh?

12 oz

$4.59 $2.99

4. The large engine has 258 horsepower. The economy engine has 92 horsepower. What is the difference in the horsepower between the two engines?

5. This year Great Rapids has 15 schools. Next year the number of schools will be reduced by 2. How many schools does the city plan to open next year?

Solving Subtraction Word Problems with Key Words

You can now complete the example in the "Finding Subtraction Key Words" lesson.

EXAMPLE 1 The large cup contains 16 ounces of soda. The small cup contains 6 ounces less than the large cup. How many ounces does the small cup contain?

> **STEP 1** *question:* How many ounces does the small cup contain?
>
> **STEP 2** *necessary information:* 16 ounces, 6 ounces
>
> **STEP 3** *subtraction key words:* less than
>
> **STEP 4** *subtract:* 16 ounces – 6 ounces = **10 ounces**

$$\begin{array}{r} 16 \\ -\ 6 \\ \hline 10 \end{array}$$

In Example 2, the key words *less* and *than* are separated.

EXAMPLE 2 How much less does a $13 polyester dress cost than a $24 cotton one?

> **STEP 1** *question:* How much less does a $13 polyester dress cost?
>
> **STEP 2** *necessary information:* $13, $24
>
> **STEP 3** *subtraction key words:* less than
>
> **STEP 4** *subtract:* $24 – $13 = **$11**

$$\begin{array}{r} 24 \\ -\ 13 \\ \hline 11 \end{array}$$

This is also an example of a common type of subtraction problem. To solve it, you must reverse the order in which the numbers appear in the problem.

In each problem below, circle the key words and do the arithmetic. Be sure to include the label as part of your answer.

1. After a tornado destroyed 36 of the 105 homes in Carson, how many homes were left?

2. How much change did Mel receive when he paid for $16 worth of gas with a $20 bill?

3. After spending $325 of the $361 in her savings account for Christmas presents, how much did Carmena have left in her account?

4. What is the difference in price between the two cars below?

$12,635 $7,849

5. In the evening, the temperature had fallen 12 degrees from the afternoon high of 86 degrees, following a morning low of 58 degrees. What is the evening temperature?

6. Harold weighs 161 pounds, and his wife Nora weighs 104 pounds. How much more does Harold weigh than Nora?

7. Yesterday the hurricane was reported to be 420 miles offshore. Overnight it came 140 miles closer. How far from shore was it at dawn?

8. Caroline's phone bill was $121 in March and $46 in April. By how much did her phone bill decrease in April?

9. After the fire, Peg discovered that out of 460 books in her personal library, only 133 remained. How many of her books were lost in the fire?

 10. Lou bought a 21-pound sirloin strip. After the butcher trimmed the fat and cut the strip into steaks, the weight of the meat was 17 pounds. How much less was the weight of the meat after the fat was trimmed?

Key Word Lists for Addition and Subtraction

Now you know that some key words may help you decide to add. Other key words may help you decide to subtract.

Here are some important key words to remember. You may want to add more words to these lists.

ADDITION KEY WORDS

sum	raise
plus	both
add	combined
and	in all
total	altogether
increase	additional
more	extra

SUBTRACTION KEY WORDS

less than	left
more than	remain
decrease	fell
difference	dropped
reduce	change
lost	
nearer	
farther }	other *-er* comparison words

Solving Addition and Subtraction Problems with Key Words

Now that you have seen how key words are used in addition and subtraction word problems, look at the following examples to see the difference between addition word problems with key words and subtraction word problems with key words.

EXAMPLE 1 It snowed 7 inches on Monday and 5 inches on Friday. What was the total amount of snow for the week?

   STEP 1 *question:* What was the total amount of snow?

   STEP 2 *necessary information:* 7 inches, 5 inches

   STEP 3 *addition key words:* and, total

   STEP 4 *add:* 7 inches + 5 inches = **12 inches**

$$\begin{array}{r} 7 \\ + 5 \\ \hline 12 \end{array}$$

EXAMPLE 2 The city usually runs its entire fleet of 237 buses during the morning rush hour. On Thursday morning, 46 buses and 13 subway cars were out of service. How many buses were left to run during the Thursday morning rush hour?

   STEP 1 *question:* How many buses were running Thursday morning?

   STEP 2 *necessary information:* 237 buses, 46 buses (13 subway cars is not necessary information.)

   STEP 3 *subtraction key word:* left

   STEP 4 *subtract:* 237 buses – 46 buses = **191 buses**

$$\begin{array}{r} 237 \\ - 46 \\ \hline 191 \end{array}$$

In addition word problems, numbers are often being combined, and you are looking for the total. In subtraction word problems, numbers are being compared, and you are looking for the difference.

In this exercise, circle the key words. Decide whether to add or to subtract. Then solve the problem.

1. A book saleswoman sold 86 books on Monday and 53 books on Tuesday. How many books did she sell altogether?

2. After selling 15 rings on Wednesday, a jeweler sold 31 rings and 4 necklaces on Thursday. How many more rings did she sell on Thursday than on Wednesday?

3. At the town meeting, votes are recorded on the vote tally board as shown at the right. What was the total vote?

Vote Tally Board	
Yes	564
No	365

4. This year the Graphics Computer Company sold 253 units. Last year it sold 421 units. By how many units did sales decrease this year?

5. Mammoth Oil advertises that with its new brand of oil, a car can be driven 10,000 miles between oil changes. With Mammoth's old oil, a car's oil had to be changed every 3,000 miles. How much farther can you drive with Mammoth's new oil than with its old oil?

6. Last year, the Gonzales family paid $530 a month for rent. If their rent was increased by $35 a month, how much monthly rent are they now paying?

7. In April the Gonzales family paid $26 for electricity. In July their bill rose to $42. How much more did they pay in July than in April?

MORE ADDITION AND SUBTRACTION WORD PROBLEMS: WHOLE NUMBERS

Key Words Can Be Misleading

So far you have seen one approach to solving word problems.

STEP 1 Find the key word.

STEP 2 Decide whether the key word suggests addition or subtraction.

STEP 3 Do the arithmetic the key word directs you to do.

This approach can work in many situations.

But Be Careful!

Sometimes the same key word that helped you decide to add in one word problem can appear in a problem that requires subtraction.

The next two examples use the *same* numbers and the *same* key words. In one problem, you must add to find the answer, while in the other, you must subtract.

EXAMPLE 1 Judy bought 4 cans of pineapple and 16 cans of applesauce. What was the total number of cans that she bought?

STEP 1 *question:* What was the total number of cans?

STEP 2 *necessary information:* 4 cans of pineapple, 16 cans of applesauce.

$$\begin{array}{r} 16 \\ + 4 \\ \hline 20 \end{array}$$

STEP 3 *key words:* and, total
Since you are looking for a total, you should add.

STEP 4 4 cans of pineapple + 16 cans of applesauce = **20 cans of fruit**

EXAMPLE 2 Judy bought a total of 16 cans of fruit. Four were cans of pineapple. The rest were applesauce. How many cans of applesauce did she buy?

> **STEP 1** *question:* How many cans of applesauce did she buy?
>
> **STEP 2** *necessary information:* 4 cans of pineapple, 16 cans of fruit
>
> **STEP 3** *key word:* total
> Since you have been given a total and are being asked to find a part of it, you must subtract.
>
> **STEP 4** 16 cans of fruit – 4 cans of pineapple = **12 cans of applesauce**

$$\begin{array}{r} 16 \\ -\ 4 \\ \hline 12 \end{array}$$

In both examples, the word *total* was used. In Example 1, the question asked you to find the total. Therefore, you had to add. But in Example 2, the total (cans of fruit) was part of the information given in the problem. The question asked you to find the number of cans of applesauce, a part of the total. To do this, you had to subtract the number of cans of pineapple from the total number of cans.

These two examples show that key words can be good clues, **but they are only a guide to understanding a word problem.** If you use the key words without understanding what you are reading, you may do the wrong arithmetic.

....

This exercise will help you to carefully examine problems containing key words. In each of the following items, the key word has been left out and the solution has been given. Two choices have been given for the missing word; circle the correct one.

1. Last week eggs cost 87 cents a dozen. This week the price _____ 9 cents. How much are eggs this week?

   87 cents + 9 cents = **96 cents**   (fell, rose)

2. Last week the price of eggs _____ to 87 cents a dozen. The price had originally been 78 cents. By how much did the eggs change in price?

   87 cents – 78 cents = **9 cents**   (fell, rose)

3. The 5% sales tax is going to _____ 1%. What will the new sales tax be?

   5% + 1% = **6%** (increase, decrease)

4. The 5% sales tax is going to _____ 1%. What will the new sales tax be?

   5% – 1% = **4%** (increase, decrease)

5. Next month, the Jones family is going to receive $14 a week _____ for food stamps. They now receive $87 a week. How much a week will they be receiving?

   $87 – $14 = **$73** (more, less)

6. The Johnson family's food stamp allotment has been cut. They now receive $14 a week _____, or $87 for stamps. What had been their original allotment for stamps?

   $87 + $14 = **$101** (more, less)

7. Gloria used to keep her thermostat at 72 degrees. To save energy, she _____ it 6 degrees. What was the new temperature in her apartment?

   72 degrees – 6 degrees = **66 degrees** (raised, lowered)

8. Jerline's mother came to visit for the weekend. To make sure that her mother was comfortable, she _____ the thermostat to 70 degrees. Usually, the thermostat is set at 66 degrees. By how much has Jerline changed the temperature?

   70 degrees – 66 degrees = **4 degrees** (lowered, raised)

9. Gail normally ate 2,400 calories a day. While on a special diet, she ate 1,100 calories _____. How many calories a day did she eat on her diet?

   2,400 calories + 1,100 calories = **3,500 calories** (more, less)

Restating the Problem

Have you ever tried to help someone else work out a word problem? Think about what you do. Often, you read the problem with the person, then discuss it or put it in your own words to help the person see what is happening. You can use this method—**restating the problem**—to help yourself solve a problem.

Restating the problem can be especially helpful when the word problem contains no key words. Look at the following example:

EXAMPLE   Susan has already driven her car 2,700 miles since its last oil change. She still plans to drive 600 miles before changing the oil. How many miles does she plan to drive between oil changes?

STEP 1   *question:* How many miles does she plan to drive between oil changes?

STEP 2   *necessary information:* 2,700 miles, 600 miles

STEP 3   Decide what arithmetic operation to use. Restate the problem in your own words: "You are given the number of miles Susan has already driven and the number of miles more that she plans to drive. You need to find the total number of miles between oil changes. You should add."

STEP 4   2,700 miles + 600 miles = **3,300 miles** between oil changes

$$\begin{array}{r} 2{,}700 \\ +600 \\ \hline 3{,}300 \end{array}$$

STEP 5   It makes sense that she will drive 3,300 miles between oil changes since you are looking for a number larger than the 2,700 miles that she has already driven.

Try this method with the next exercise. Read the problem, and then restate it to yourself. In future work with particularly confusing word problems, you should try this method of talking to yourself to understand the problems.

Each word problem is followed by two short explanations. One gives you a reason to add to find the answer. The other gives you a reason to subtract to find the answer. Circle the correct explanation. DO NOT SOLVE!

1. Margi's weekly food budget has increased $12 over last year's to $87 per week. How much had she spent per week for food last year?

   a. The budget has increased since last year. Therefore, you add the two numbers.
   b. Her food budget has increased over last year's. The new, larger budget is given. Therefore, you subtract to find last year's smaller amount.

2. In the runoff election for mayor, Fritz Neptune got 14,662 votes, and Julio Cortez got 17,139 votes. How many votes were cast in the election?

   a. To find the total number of votes cast, you should add the two numbers given.
   b. To find the number of votes cast, you should subtract to find the difference between the two numbers.

3. The difference between first class (the most expensive fare) and the coach air fare is $68. If coach costs $212, how much does first class cost?

   a. To find the cost of first class, you subtract to find the difference between the two fares.
   b. First class costs more than coach. Since you are looking for the larger fare, you add the smaller fare to the difference between the two fares.

4. It costs $66,840 to run and maintain the town's pool. During the year, $59,176 was collected from user fees for the pool, and the town government paid the rest of the cost. How much money did the town government have to pay?

   a. To find the total cost, you add the cost of running and maintaining the pool to the amount collected in user fees.
   b. You are given the total cost of running the pool and the part of the cost covered by user fees. To find the cost to the town government, you subtract.

5. After reading a 320-page novel, Danyel read a 205-page history book. How many pages did Danyel read?

   a. Since you are looking for the total number of pages, you add.
   b. To find the difference between the number of pages in the two books, you subtract.

6. After making 24 bowls, Claire made 16 plates. How many pieces did she make?

   a. Since the number of pieces includes the number of bowls and plates, you add them together.
   b. Since you are looking for a difference, you subtract the number of plates from the number of bowls.

7. A factory has produced 48,624 microwave ovens so far this year. The company expects to produce 37,716 microwave ovens during the rest of the year. What is the projected production of ovens for the year?

   a. To find the projected production for the year, you subtract the number of microwave ovens to be produced from the number of ovens that have been produced so far.
   b. To find the projected production for the entire year, you add the number of ovens already produced to the number of ovens that are expected to be produced.

8. Diane has a 50,000-mile warranty on her car. The car has gone 34,913 miles. As of today, how many miles will the car have left on its warranty?

   a. To find the total number of miles that the car has left on its warranty, you add the number of miles Diane has driven to the number of miles that the warranty covers.
   b. Since Diane has driven on the warranty, you subtract the miles she has already driven from the mileage that the warranty covers.

Using Pictures and Diagrams to Solve Word Problems

Another approach that people use to solve word problems is to form a picture of the problem. While some people can do this in their heads, many people find it very useful to draw a picture or diagram of the problem.

EXAMPLE 1 A recipe for 48 ounces of punch calls for 23 ounces of fruit juice and liquor. The rest is club soda. How much of the recipe is club soda?

STEP 1 *question:* How much of the recipe is club soda?

STEP 2 *necessary information:* 48 ounces of punch, 23 ounces of fruit juice and liquor

STEP 3 Draw a diagram, and decide whether to add or subtract.

The diagram shows that you can find the remaining contents by subtraction.

punch – fruit juice and liquor = club soda

23 oz juice and liquor

? oz club soda

48 oz total

STEP 4 Do the arithmetic.

48 oz – 23 oz = **25 oz**

STEP 5 Make sure that your answer is sensible. It makes sense that the number of ounces of club soda is less than the number of ounces of punch.

EXAMPLE 2 After losing $237 at the blackjack table, Yolanda had $63 left for spending money for the rest of her vacation. How much spending money had she brought with her?

STEP 1 *question:* How much spending money had she brought with her?

STEP 2 *necessary information:* $237 lost, $63 left

STEP 3 Draw a diagram, and decide whether to add or subtract.

The diagram shows that you can find the total spending money by addition.

$ lost + $ left = total $ spending money

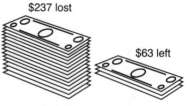

$237 lost

$63 left

$? total brought on trip

STEP 4 Do the arithmetic.

$237 + $63 = **$300**

STEP 5 Make sure that your answer is sensible. Since she lost money, it makes sense that Yolanda started with more money than she has now.

EXAMPLE 3 The oil tanker *Whyon* was loaded with 150,000 barrels of crude oil when it struck a reef and spilled most of its oil. Within a week, the cleanup crew had pumped all the remaining oil from the tanker. If the cleanup crew pumped 97,416 barrels of oil from the ship, how many barrels of oil were spilled?

STEP 1 *question:* How many barrels of oil were spilled?

STEP 2 *necessary information:* 150,000 barrels of crude oil, 97,416 barrels of crude oil

STEP 3 Draw a diagram, and decide whether to add or subtract.

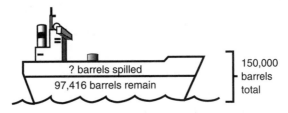

The diagram shows that you can find the amount spilled by subtraction.

total load – amount left = amount spilled

STEP 4 Do the arithmetic.

$$\begin{array}{r} 150{,}000 \text{ barrels} \\ - \ 97{,}416 \text{ barrels} \\ \hline \mathbf{52{,}584} \text{ \textbf{barrels}} \end{array}$$

STEP 5 Make sure that your answer is sensible. It makes sense that the amount spilled is less than the total amount of oil that was originally on the tanker.

⋯⋯⋯⋯⋯⋯⋯⋯⋯⋯⋯⋯⋯⋯⋯⋯⋯⋯⋯⋯⋯⋯⋯⋯⋯

For each problem, make a drawing or a diagram and decide whether to add or subtract. Then solve the problem.

1. If three more students are added to this class, we will have 31 students. How many students do we have now?

2. Rafael Hernandez paid $39 less in taxes in 1998 than in 1999. He paid $483 in 1998. How much did he pay in 1999?

3. Every hour 12,000 gallons of water flow through the dam spillway. The 41-year-old dam operator plans to decrease the flow by 3,500 gallons an hour. What will be the new rate of water flow?

4. A $120 ink-jet printer costs $359 less than a laser printer. How much does the laser printer cost?

5. An ink-jet printer costs $120 less than a $359 laser printer. How much does the ink-jet printer cost?

6. Between 6 P.M. and 11 P.M., the temperature decreased by 13 degrees to 61 degrees. What had the temperature been at 6 P.M.?

7. At 6 P.M. the temperature was 61 degrees. Between 6 P.M. and 11 P.M., it decreased 13 degrees. What was the temperature at 11 P.M.?

8. In 1938 1,412 people graduated from Lincoln High School. Today, 457 of these graduates are still living. How many of the graduates have died?

9. Marion took out a loan for $6,000. She has paid back $3,800. How much does she still owe?

10. A 2,600-pound truck can carry a 1,000-pound load. How much does the fully loaded truck weigh?

11. Gamma Airlines allows each passenger to check a maximum of two bags that together must weigh less than 70 pounds. At check-in, Khanh's bags weighed 24 pounds and 42 pounds. Did the total weight of her bags exceed the weight limit?

12. Macrohard Corporation sold 790,000 copies of their game software Fog. They estimate that there are 600,000 illegal copies of Fog. If their estimates are correct, how many copies of Fog exist?

Using Number Sentences to Solve Word Problems

Addition and subtraction word problems can be solved by writing number sentences. A **number sentence** restates a word problem first in words and then in numbers.

EXAMPLE 1   Lori went to school for 5 years in Levittown before moving to Plainview. She then went to school for 7 years in Plainview. For how many years did she go to school?

To write a number sentence, first write the information in the problem in words.

Levittown plus Plainview equals total years

Then substitute numbers and mathematical symbols for the words.

5 years + 7 years = total years

Solve.

$$\begin{array}{r} 5 \\ +\,7 \\ \hline 12 \end{array}$$

12 years = total years

EXAMPLE 2   A play ran for two nights at a theater seating 270 people. The first night 235 people saw the play, and 261 people saw the play the second night. How many people saw the play during its two-night run?

STEP 1   *question:* How many people saw the play during its two-night run?

STEP 2   *necessary information:* 235 people, 261 people

STEP 3   *number sentence:*

first night + second night = total people
235 people + 261 people = total people

$$\begin{array}{r} 235 \\ +\,261 \\ \hline 496 \end{array}$$

STEP 4   **496 people = total people**

EXAMPLE 3   Gloria bought a $57 dress on sale for $19. How much did she save?

STEP 1   *question:* How much did she save?

STEP 2   *necessary information:* $57, $19

STEP 3   *number sentence:*

original price − sale price = savings
$57 − $19 = savings

$$\begin{array}{r} 57 \\ -\,19 \\ \hline 38 \end{array}$$

STEP 4   **$38 = savings**

Underline the necessary information. Write a word sentence and a number sentence. Then solve the problem.

1. Ross needed a 20-cent stamp. If he paid for the stamp with a quarter, how much change did he get?

2. Bruce drives 32 miles to work each day. When he arrived at work on Monday, he found that he had driven 51 miles that day. How many additional miles over his regular commuting distance had Bruce driven on Monday?

3. The theater company needs to sell 172 Saturday tickets to break even. How many more Saturday tickets must they sell in order to break even according to the chart at the right?

Ticket Sales	
Thursday	120
Friday	145
Saturday	134

4. Wendy decided to buy a $3,300 used car. She had saved $1,460. She got a loan for the rest. What was the amount of the loan?

5. Becci Bachman needs 150 names on her nominating petition to run for office. She collected 119 names on her first day of campaigning. How many more names does she have to collect?

6. After losing 47 pounds, Ann weighed 119. What was her original weight?

7. Lucy's monthly food stamp allotment was reduced by $13 to $168. How much was she getting in food stamps before the reduction?

8. The refrigerator shown at the right was marked down to $379. How much did Kathy save by buying the refrigerator on sale?

$465

9. John had $213 withheld for federal income tax. In fact, he only owed $185. How much of a refund will he receive?

10. A car factory cut production by 3,500 cars to 8,200 cars a month. What had the monthly production been before the cutback?

 11. Maria earned $28,682 last year. She spent $27,991. How much did she save?

 12. Mr. Crockett's cow Bertha produced 1,423 gallons of milk last year. His other cow, Calico, produced 1,289 gallons. How much milk did his cows produce last year?

 13. Memorial Stadium has 72,070 seats. At the football game, 58,682 people had seats. How many seats were empty?

14. In one garden bed, a gardener grew spinach. When the spinach was harvested, he grew green beans. The spinach was harvested after 49 days. The green beans were harvested after 56 days. For how many days were vegetables growing in the garden bed?

ADDITION AND SUBTRACTION WORD PROBLEMS: DECIMALS AND FRACTIONS

Using the Substitution Method

So far, you have solved addition and subtraction word problems using whole numbers. However, many students worry when they see word problems using large whole numbers, fractions, or decimals.

Read the following examples and think about their differences and similarities.

EXAMPLE 1   A cardboard manufacturer makes cardboard 4 millimeters thick. To save money, he plans to make cardboard 3 millimeters thick instead. How much thinner is the new cardboard?

STEP 1   *question:* How much thinner is the new cardboard?

STEP 2   *necessary information:* 4 mm, 3 mm

STEP 3   Decide what arithmetic operation to use. You are given the thickness of each piece of cardboard. Since you must find the difference between the two pieces, you should subtract.

$$\begin{array}{r} 4 \\ -\ 3 \\ \hline 1 \end{array}$$

STEP 4   4 mm − 3 mm = **1 mm**

> **Note:** *mm* stands for *millimeter.* You should be able to do this type of problem even if you aren't familiar with the units of measurement.

EXAMPLE 2   A cardboard manufacturer makes cardboard 6.45 millimeters thick. To save money, he plans to make cardboard 5.5 millimeters thick instead. How much thinner is the new cardboard?

STEP 1   *question:* How much thinner is the new cardboard?

STEP 2   *necessary information:* 6.45 mm, 5.5 mm

STEP 3   Decide what arithmetic operation to use. You are given the thickness of each piece of cardboard. Since you must find the difference between the two pieces, you should subtract. Be sure to put the decimal points one under the other.

$$\begin{array}{r} 6.45 \\ -\ 5.50 \\ \hline 0.95 \end{array}$$

STEP 4   6.45 mm − 5.50 mm = **0.95 mm**

EXAMPLE 3 A cardboard manufacturer makes cardboard $\frac{3}{8}$ inch thick. To save money, he plans to make cardboard $\frac{1}{3}$ inch thick instead. How much thinner is the new cardboard?

  STEP 1 *question:* How much thinner is the new cardboard?

  STEP 2 *necessary information:* $\frac{3}{8}$ inch, $\frac{1}{3}$ inch

  STEP 3 Decide what arithmetic operation to use. You are given the thickness of each piece of cardboard. Since you must find the difference between the two pieces, you should subtract.

  STEP 4 $\frac{3}{8}$ in. $- \frac{1}{3}$ in. $= \frac{1}{24}$ **in.**

$$\frac{3}{8} = \frac{9}{24}$$
$$-\frac{1}{3} = \frac{8}{24}$$
$$\overline{\qquad\frac{1}{24}}$$

> **Note:** Remember, to find the solution, you must change unlike fractions to fractions with a common denominator.

What did you notice about the three example problems?

The wording of all three is exactly the same. Only the numbers and labels have been changed. All three problems are solved the same way, by subtracting.

Then why do Examples 2 and 3 seem harder than the first example?

The difficulty has to do with **math intuition,** or the feel that a person has for numbers. You have a very clear idea of the correct answer to $4 - 3$. It is more difficult to picture $7,483,251 + 29,983$ or $6.45 - 5.5$. And for most of us, our intuition totally breaks down for $\frac{3}{8} - \frac{1}{3}$.

Changing only the numbers in a word problem does not change what must be done to solve the problem. By substituting small whole numbers in a problem, you can understand the problem and how to solve it.

EXAMPLE 4 A floor is to be covered with a layer of $\frac{3}{4}$-inch fiberboard and $\frac{7}{16}$-inch plywood. By how much will the floor level be raised?

Fractions, especially those with different denominators, are especially hard to picture. You can make the problem easier to understand by substituting small whole numbers for the fractions. You can substitute any numbers, but try to use numbers under 10. These numbers do not have to look like the numbers they are replacing.

In Example 4, try substituting 3 for $\frac{3}{4}$ and 2 for $\frac{7}{16}$. The problem now looks like this:

> A floor is to be covered by a layer of 3-inch fiberboard and 2-inch plywood. By how much will the floor level be raised?

You can now read this problem and know that you must add.

Once you make your decision about *how* to solve the problem, you can return the original numbers to the word problem and work out the solution. With the substituted numbers, you decided to *add* 3 and 2. Therefore, in the original, you must *add* $\frac{3}{4}$ and $\frac{7}{16}$.

$$\frac{3}{4} = \frac{12}{16}$$
$$+\frac{7}{16} = \frac{7}{16}$$
$$\frac{19}{16} = 1\frac{3}{16} \text{ inches}$$

Remember: Choosing the whole numbers 3 and 2 was completely arbitrary. You could have used any small whole numbers.

Below is a set of six substitutions. Each of the substitutions will fit only one of the following six word problems. Match the letter of the correct substitution to each problem. (After each problem, you are told which numbers to substitute for that problem. To keep it simple, we are only using the numbers 4, 3, and 1 in the substitutions.)

a. 3 pounds + 4 pounds = 7 pounds
b. 4 pounds − 3 pounds = 1 pound
c. $3 − $1 = $2
d. $3 + $1 = $4
e. 3 inches + 1 inch = 4 inches
f. 3 inches − 1 inch = 2 inches

1. A sweater that normally sells for $35.99 has been marked down by $10.99. What is the sale price of the sweater?

   Substitute $3 for $35.99 and $1 for $10.99.

   _____

2. How much heavier is the rump roast than the round roast shown at the right?

   Substitute 3 for 3.46 and 4 for 4.17.

   _____

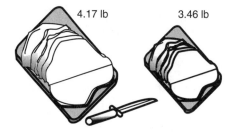

4.17 lb   3.46 lb

3. Robin bought a 3.28-pound steak and a 4.84-pound chicken. What was the weight of the meat she bought?

   Substitute 3 for 3.28 and 4 for 4.84.

   _____

4. Janice bought a skirt for $31.99 and a slip for $11.59. How much did she spend in all?

   Substitute $3 for $31.99 and $1 for $11.59.

   _____

5. Michael caught a $21\frac{1}{4}$-inch fish. His friend Paul caught a $23\frac{1}{16}$-inch fish. How much longer was Paul's fish?

   Substitute 1 for $21\frac{1}{4}$ and 3 for $23\frac{1}{16}$.

   _____

6. Two boards were placed end-to-end. The first board was $40\frac{7}{8}$ inches long. The second board was $32\frac{3}{4}$ inches long. What was the combined length of the 2 boards?

   Substitute 3 for $40\frac{7}{8}$ and 1 for $32\frac{3}{4}$.

   _____

Using Estimation

When your car is in an accident and you take it to an auto body shop for repairs, you first receive an **estimate** for the cost of the repairs. This might not be the exact or final price, but it should be close.

When solving word problems, it is also important to have some idea of what the answer should be before you start doing the arithmetic. You can get an estimate of the answer by approximating the numbers in the problem.

An **estimate** is almost, but not quite, the exact number. For instance,

> In the last election, the newspaper reported that Alderman Jones received 52% of the vote and his opponent received 48%. Actually, the alderman received 52.1645% of the vote and his opponent received 47.8355%.

The newspaper did not report the exact percent of the vote; it **rounded** the numbers to the nearest whole percent. Rounded numbers are one type of estimate.

Estimating the numbers and doing quick arithmetic in your head is a good way to check your work. Throughout the rest of this workbook, you should first estimate a solution before doing the calculation. The estimation icon will indicate that the problem is best solved by rounding and estimating.

Below is a set of six estimated solutions. The numbers in the solutions have been rounded. Match each word problem with one of the solutions.

a. 9 miles − 7 miles = 2 miles
b. 9 miles + 7 miles = 16 miles
c. 4 billion dollars − 1 billion dollars = 3 billion dollars
d. 4 billion dollars + 1 billion dollars = 5 billion dollars
e. 37,000 fans − 35,000 fans = 2,000 fans
f. 37,000 fans + 35,000 fans = 72,000 fans

1. During the last weekend in July, 35,142 fans saw a baseball game on Saturday. On Sunday 36,994 fans saw a game. What was the total attendance for the weekend?

   _____

2. Nationwide, Grand Discount stores sold 37,238 window fans in April and 34,982 fans in May. How many more fans were sold in April?

   _____

3. The original estimate for the cost of a nuclear power plant was .984 billion dollars. The final cost was 4.16 billion dollars. How much did the price increase from the original estimate?

   _____

4. The state budget is 3.92 billion dollars. It is expected to increase 1.2 billion dollars over the next 5 years. How much is the budget expected to be 5 years from now?

   _____

5. By expressway, it is $7\frac{1}{4}$ miles to the beach. By back roads, it is $8\frac{9}{10}$ miles. How much shorter is the trip when driving by expressway?

   _____

6. Pat is a long-distance runner. He ran $6\frac{9}{10}$ miles on Saturday and $9\frac{1}{8}$ miles on Sunday. How many miles in all did he run during the weekend?

   _____

Decimals: Restating the Problem

Restating the problem is one method that will work as well with solving decimal problems as with whole-number problems. Don't worry about the decimal points until after you have decided to add or subtract. Then, remember to line up the decimal points before doing the arithmetic.

EXAMPLE   A pair of pants was on sale for $8.99. A shirt was on sale for $6.49. Alan decided to buy both. How much did he spend?

STEP 1   *question:* How much did he spend?

STEP 2   *necessary information:* $8.99, $6.49

STEP 3   *restatement:* Since Alan is buying both items, you add to find the total amount he spent.

STEP 4 $8.99 + $6.49 = **$15.48**

STEP 5   Round $8.99 to $9 and $6.49 to $6.

$9 + $6 = $15

Therefore, your answer should be close to $15. Making an estimate is a good method of checking your answer and making sure it is sensible.

$$8.99$$
$$+\ 6.49$$
$$\overline{15.48}$$

Circle the letter of the correct restatement and solve the problem. Use estimation to make sure your answer is sensible.

1. Using his odometer, George discovered that one route to work was 6.3 miles long and the other was 7.1 miles. How much shorter was the first way?

    a. Since you are given the two distances to work, add to find out how much shorter the first way was.
    b. To find how much shorter the first way was, subtract to find the difference.

2. Max had to put gasoline in his 8-year-old car twice last week. The first time, he put in 9.4 gallons. The second time, he put in 14.7 gallons. How much gasoline did he put in his car last week?

    a. To find the total amount of gasoline he put in his car, you add.
    b. Since you are given the two amounts of gasoline, you subtract to find the difference.

3. The first fish fillet weighed 1.42 pounds. The second fillet weighed 0.98 pound. Alice decided to buy both fillets. What was the weight of the fish she bought?

    a. To find the total weight of the two fish fillets, you add.
    b. Since you are given the weight of the two fish fillets, you subtract to find the difference between their weights.

4. At the Reckless Speedway, Bobby was clocked at 198.7 mph, while Mario was clocked at 200.15 mph. How much faster did Mario drive than Bobby?

    a. Add the two speeds to find how much faster Mario drove.
    b. Since Mario drove faster, subtract Bobby's speed from his to find out the difference between the speeds.

5. Last year the unemployment rate was 7.9%. This year it has increased to 9.1%. By how much did unemployment rise?

    a. To find how much unemployment rose, add the two unemployment rates.
    b. To find the rise in unemployment, subtract last year's rate from this year's rate.

Decimals: Drawings and Diagrams

Diagrams and drawings can help you solve decimal addition or subtraction word problems.

EXAMPLE A metal bearing was 0.24 centimeters thick. The machinist ground it down until it was 0.065 centimeters thinner. How thick was the metal bearing after it had been ground down?

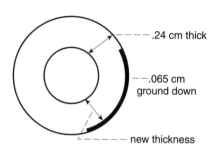

.24 cm thick

.065 cm ground down

new thickness

STEP 1 *question:* How thick was the metal bearing after it had been ground down?

STEP 2 *necessary information:* 0.24 cm, 0.065 cm

STEP 3 *make a drawing:* To find the size of the bearing after it was ground down, you subtract.

STEP 4 Do the arithmetic. Be sure to line up the decimal points. If you add a zero, you can see that 0.24 (0.240) is larger than 0.065.

$$\begin{array}{r} 0.240 \\ -\ 0.065 \\ \hline 0.175 \end{array}$$

0.240 cm − 0.065 cm = **0.175 cm**

> **Remember:** When subtracting decimals, first line up the decimal points. Then fill any blank spaces to the right of the decimal point with zeros. This should help you borrow correctly.

Make a drawing or a diagram, and solve the problem. (Each person's drawing may be different. What is important is that the diagram makes sense to you.)

1. Meatball subs used to cost $2.60 at Mike's, but he just raised the price $0.25. How much do meatball subs cost now?

2. Tara's prescription for 0.55 gram of antibiotic was not strong enough. Her doctor gave her a new prescription for 0.7 gram of antibiotic. How much stronger was the new prescription?

3. Mike Johnson was hitting .342 before he went into a batting slump. By the end of his slump, his average had dropped .083. What was his batting average at the end of his slump?

4. Joyce earned $313.50 and had $126.13 taken out for deductions. How much was her take-home pay?

5. A wooden peg is 1.6 inches wide and 3.2 inches long. It can be squeezed into an opening 0.05 inch smaller than the width of the peg. What is the width of the opening?

6. By midweek Wendy had spent $46.65. At the end of the week, she had spent $23.35 more. How much did Wendy spend that week?

7. The gap of a spark plug should be 0.08 inch. The plug would still work if the gap were off by as much as 0.015 inch. What is the largest gap that would still work?

8. The King Coal Company mined 126.4 tons of coal. Because of high sulfur content, 18.64 tons of coal were unusable. How many tons of coal were usable?

9. Bonnie was mixing chemicals in a lab. The formula called for 1.45 milliliters of sulfuric acid, but she had 1.8 milliliters of sulfuric acid in her pipette. How much extra sulfuric acid does she have in the pipette? (A pipette is a glass tube used for measuring chemicals.)

10. Barbara complained that the 2.64-pound steak had too much excess fat. The butcher trimmed the steak and reweighed it. It now weighed 2.1 pounds. How much fat did the butcher cut off the steak?

Decimals: Writing Number Sentences

Number sentences can help you solve decimal addition and subtraction word problems. Look at the following examples to see how number sentences are used.

EXAMPLE 1 Meryl bought $16.27 worth of groceries and paid with a $20 bill. How much change did she receive?

  STEP 1 *question:* How much change did she receive?

  STEP 2 *necessary information:* $16.27, $20

  STEP 3 *number sentence:*

$$\begin{array}{r} \$20.00 \\ -\$16.27 \\ \hline \$\ 3.73 \end{array}$$

  amount paid − price of groceries = change
  $20.00 − $16.27 = change

  STEP 4 **$3.73 = change**

EXAMPLE 2 On sale a pair of pants costs $22.49. They had been discounted $4.49 from the original price. What was the original price?

  STEP 1 *question:* What was the original price?

  STEP 2 *necessary information:* $4.49, $22.49

  STEP 3 *number sentence:*

$$\begin{array}{r} \$22.49 \\ +\$\ 4.49 \\ \hline \$26.98 \end{array}$$

  sale price + discount = original price
  $22.49 + $4.49 = original price

  STEP 4 **$26.98 = original price**

Underline the necessary information. Write a word sentence and a number sentence. Then solve the problem.

1. The Sticky Candy Company decided to reduce the size of their chocolate candy bar by 0.6 ounce to 2.4 ounces. How much did their chocolate bar weigh before the change?

2. Julie's lunch cost $3.38. If she paid with a $10 bill, how much change did she get?

3. Bernice bought one chicken that weighed 3.94 pounds and one that weighed 4.68 pounds. She also bought a 1.32-pound steak. How much chicken did she buy?

4. The odometer at the right shows Mark's car mileage when he left Boston. When he arrived in New York, the odometer read 23,391.4 miles. How long was the trip?

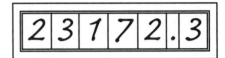

5. The chart at the right shows the costs of subway and bus rides in Connie's city. If Connie needs to take one bus and one subway to her mother's house, how much will it cost her for a one-way trip?

Fares	
Bus	$.40
Subway	$.65

6. Judy spent $341.98 for a new washing machine in Massachusetts. If she had bought the same machine in New Hampshire, she would have paid $335.26, since that state does not have a sales tax. How much less would she have paid in New Hampshire?

7. When he ran the 200-meter race, Marcus ran the first 100 meters in 14.36 seconds and the second 100 meters in 13.9 seconds. What was his total time for the race?

8. One assembly line at the plant produced 966 soda bottles in one hour. Another line produced 50 fewer bottles in the same amount of time. How many bottles did the second line produce in an hour?

Fractions: Restating the Problem

In this section, you will restate the problem in order to decide whether to add or subtract. Before solving these fraction problems, you might want to use estimation to help you decide what arithmetic operation to use.

EXAMPLE   Tanya grew $2\frac{3}{4}$ inches last year. If she was $42\frac{1}{2}$ inches tall a year ago, how tall is she now?

STEP 1   *question:* How tall is she now?

STEP 2   *necessary information:* $2\frac{3}{4}$ inches, $42\frac{1}{2}$ inches

STEP 3   *restatement:* Since you know Tanya's old height, and you know that she grew, you must add to find her new height.

STEP 4   *estimation:* 3 inches + 43 inches = 46 inches

STEP 5 $2\frac{3}{4}$ inches + $42\frac{1}{2}$ inches = height now

$2\frac{3}{4} + 42\frac{2}{4} = 44\frac{5}{4}$ inches = **$45\frac{1}{4}$ inches now**

$$2\frac{3}{4} = 2\frac{3}{4}$$
$$+\ 42\frac{1}{2} = 42\frac{2}{4}$$
$$\overline{\qquad\qquad 44\frac{5}{4} = 45\frac{1}{4}}$$

> **Remember:** Whenever you add or subtract fractions, find a common denominator.

Each problem is followed by two restatements and estimations. Circle the correct restatement. Then solve the problem.

1. A carpenter needed one piece of molding $28\frac{1}{2}$ inches long and a second piece $31\frac{1}{4}$ inches long. How much molding did he need?

    a.   To find out how much molding is needed, you should subtract.

    31 inches – 29 inches = 2 inches

    b.   To find the total amount of molding needed, you should add.

    29 inches + 31 inches = 60 inches

2. Vera combined $1\frac{2}{3}$ cups of flour and $1\frac{1}{3}$ cups of butter in a 2-quart mixing bowl. How many cups of the mixture did Vera have?

    a. Since Vera is combining the flour and butter, the amount of the mixture can be found by adding.

       2 cups + 1 cup = 3 cups

    b. Since you are given the amount of flour and the amount of butter, you subtract to find the amount of the mixture.

       2 cups – 1 cup = 1 cup

3. According to the scales at the right, how much heavier is Tara than Erin?

Tara
$71\frac{1}{4}$

Erin
$62\frac{1}{2}$

    a. Since you are comparing two weights, subtract to find the difference.

       71 pounds – 63 pounds = 8 pounds

    b. Since you are finding Tara's total weight, add the given weights.

       71 pounds + 63 pounds = 134 pounds

4. Mira was $18\frac{3}{4}$ inches tall at birth. Six months later, she was $23\frac{1}{4}$ inches tall. How much taller was Mira after 6 months than at birth?

    a. To find how much taller Mira is, add the given heights.

       19 inches + 23 inches = 42 inches

    b. To find how much taller Mira is, subtract her birth height from her height at 6 months.

       23 inches – 19 inches = 4 inches

Fractions: Diagrams and Pictures

Making diagrams and pictures can also help you solve fraction addition or subtraction word problems.

EXAMPLE   Using a $\frac{3}{8}$-inch drill bit, Judy drilled a hole that was slightly too small. She used the next size drill bit, one that was $\frac{1}{32}$ inch larger, to enlarge the hole. What was the size of the new drill bit?

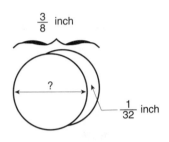

$\frac{3}{8}$ inch

$\frac{1}{32}$ inch

STEP 1   *question:* What was the size of the new drill bit?

STEP 2   *necessary information:* $\frac{3}{8}$ inch, $\frac{1}{32}$ inch

STEP 3   Decide what arithmetic operation to use. Draw a picture. Since you are looking for the next larger size, you should add.

STEP 4 $\frac{3}{8}$ inch $+ \frac{1}{32}$ inch $= \frac{12}{32}$ inch $+ \frac{1}{32}$ inch $= \frac{13}{32}$ **inch**

$$\begin{array}{r} \frac{3}{8} = \frac{12}{32} \\ + \frac{1}{32} = \frac{1}{32} \\ \hline \frac{13}{32} \end{array}$$

Make a drawing or diagram and solve each of the problems below.

1. A piece of wood called a 2-by-4 (a 2-inch by 4-inch board) is really not 4 inches wide. It is actually $\frac{5}{8}$ inch narrower. What is the real width of the board?

2. Pat is at the hospital for a total of $8\frac{1}{2}$ hours a day. If during each day he has $1\frac{3}{4}$ hours for breaks, how long does he work each day?

3. Hope worked $6\frac{1}{2}$ hours and took an additional $\frac{3}{4}$ hour for lunch. What was the total amount of time that Hope spent at work and lunch?

4. A 2-by-4 is not really 2 inches thick. It is $\frac{1}{2}$ inch thinner. What is the real thickness of the board?

5. A recipe called for $2\frac{1}{2}$ cups of flour. George only had $1\frac{2}{3}$ cups. How much flour did he borrow from his neighbor?

6. Felix tried to loosen a bolt with a $\frac{3}{4}$-inch wrench, but it was slightly too large. He decided to try the next smaller size, which was $\frac{1}{16}$ inch smaller. What was the size of the next smaller size wrench?

Fractions: Using Number Sentences

Number sentences can also help you solve fraction addition or subtraction word problems.

EXAMPLE   David planned to make a 3-inch-thick insulated roof. The roof will be made with a layer of thermal board on top of $\frac{5}{8}$-inch plywood. How thick can the thermal board be?

STEP 1   *question:* How thick can the thermal board be?

STEP 2   *necessary information:* 3 inches, $\frac{5}{8}$ inch

STEP 3   *number sentence:*

thickness of roof – plywood = thermal board

3 inches – $\frac{5}{8}$ inch = thermal board

STEP 4   **$2\frac{3}{8}$ inches = thermal board**

$$3 = 2\frac{8}{8}$$
$$-\frac{5}{8} = \frac{5}{8}$$
$$\overline{\quad 2\frac{3}{8}\quad}$$

Write a word sentence and a number sentence for each problem. Then solve the word problems.

1. Beverly filled a 3-quart punch bowl with punch. If she used $1\frac{1}{4}$ quarts of rum, how many quarts of other ingredients did she use?

2. Amy bought a skirt that was the length shown below. If she shortened it to $32\frac{3}{4}$ inches, how much did she take off?

    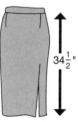
    $34\frac{1}{2}$"

3. After 3 weeks in the store, a bolt of cloth that had originally been 20 yards long was $6\frac{1}{2}$ yards long. Then $3\frac{2}{3}$ more yards of the cloth were sold. How much cloth was left?

4. Last winter Fred used $\frac{1}{8}$ cord of wood one week and $\frac{1}{12}$ cord of wood the next week to heat his house. How much wood did he use during the 2 weeks?

5. Linda bought $62\frac{1}{2}$ inches of cloth to make drapes. She used $\frac{3}{4}$ inch for the hem. How long were the drapes?

Using Algebra to Solve Word Problems

You have already seen how to use number sentences to solve addition and subtraction word problems. In algebra, instead of using words, you use a letter of the alphabet to stand for the number you are looking for.

A **number sentence** in which one amount is equal to another amount is called an **equation.** To find what number will make an equation true, you must solve the equation. One way to solve an equation is shown in the following example.

EXAMPLE   A cup of 2% milk contains 130 calories, of which 45 calories are from fat. How many calories in the cup of 2% milk are not from fat?

STEP 1   *question:* How many calories in the cup of 2% milk are not from fat?

STEP 2   *necessary information:* 130 calories, 45 calories

STEP 3   *number sentence or equation:*

calories from fat + calories not from fat = total calories
45 calories + calories not from fat = 130 calories

You can rewrite the number sentence using the letter c to stand for *calories not from fat.* (You can select any letter, but c is a good choice since it is the first letter of *calories.*) 45 calories + c = 130 calories

STEP 4   *solve the equation:*

One way to solve the equation is to subtract 45 calories from each side so that c stands alone on the left side of the equation. You can do this because if you subtract the same amount from both sides of an equation, the results are still equal.

$$
\begin{array}{rcl}
45 \text{ calories} + c & = & 130 \text{ calories} \\
- 45 \text{ calories} & = & - 45 \text{ calories} \\
\hline
c & = & 85 \text{ calories}
\end{array}
$$

STEP 5   *Does the answer make sense?*

45 calories + 85 calories = 130 calories. The answer makes sense.

Estimation: The letter is a placeholder for a number. You need to find the number that will make the equation true. To build your math intuition, try to substitute a number for the letter before you start the formal solution. Try to get a good estimate of the answer before doing the detailed calculations.

Write a word sentence and an equation for each problem. Then solve the word problem.

1. In January the adult education student Website on the Internet had 2,917 hits or visits. On February the site had 4,348 hits. How many more hits did the site have in February?

2. Belquis has a new home computer and went shopping for educational software for her son, Jonathan. She bought Math Mania for $9.98 and paid for it with a $20 bill. What was her change?

3. A slice of cheese pizza has 134 calories. A slice of pepperoni pizza has 149 calories. How many calories are in the pepperoni on a pepperoni pizza?

4. In order to patch a water-damaged post, Raymonde needed a $1\frac{3}{4}$ foot long $1'' \times 6''$ board. In her basement, she found a $3\frac{1}{2}$ foot long $1'' \times 6''$ board. After she cut the board to make the repair, how much was left over?

5. A tablet of Excedrin contains 250 milligrams of acetaminophen, 250 milligrams of aspirin, and 65 milligrams of caffeine as active ingredients. How many milligrams of active ingredients are in a tablet of Excedrin?

6. In the fleece mill, inspector Diogenes found that the pile height of a batch of fabric was $\frac{5}{8}$ inch. The standard pile height for the fabric was $\frac{7}{16}$ inch. How much material needs to be sheared off for the fabric to meet the standard?

Solving Addition and Subtraction Word Problems

Solve each problem and circle the letter of the correct answer. If the correct answer is not one of the choices, circle e. none of the above.

1. The Hammerhead Nail Company produces 55,572 nails and 4,186 screws a day. On Monday 1,263 nails were no good. How many good nails were made on Monday?

   a. 56,835 nails
   b. 54,309 nails
   c. 59,758 nails
   d. 51,386 nails
   e. 58,495 nails

2. Ana Marie had $75.62 in her wallet. How much money did she have after spending $38.56?

   a. $114.18
   b. $37.06
   c. $1.98
   d. $71.76
   e. none of the above

3. The gauges at the right show Ron's mileage using different types of gas. How much better was his mileage when he used gasohol?

   a. 4.13 miles
   b. 29 miles
   c. 41.3 miles per gallon
   d. 2.9 miles per gallon
   e. 1.15 miles per gallon

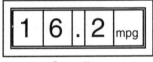

Gasoline

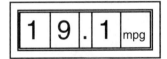

Gasohol

4. When Kathy bought her car, she paid $1,800 down and had $640 left in her savings account. She then paid $6,400 over the next 2 years to finish paying for the car. How much did the car cost her?

   a. $8,840
   b. $4,600
   c. $4,100
   d. $8,200
   e. $7,560

5. Before cooking, a hamburger weighed $\frac{1}{4}$ pound. After cooking, it weighed $\frac{3}{16}$ pound. The rest of the hamburger was fat that burned off during cooking. How much fat burned off during cooking?

   a. $\frac{4}{20}$ pound

   b. $\frac{1}{6}$ pound

   c. $\frac{1}{16}$ pound

   d. $\frac{7}{16}$ pound

   e. none of the above

6. Brand X contains 0.47 gram of pain reliever per 1.5-gram tablet. Brand Y contains 0.6 gram of pain reliever. How much more pain reliever does Brand Y have than Brand X?

   a. 0.53 gram
   b. 0.41 gram
   c. 0.13 gram
   d. 0.27 gram
   e. 2.57 grams

7. A public television station has already raised $391,445 and must raise $528,555 more to stay in business. What was the target amount for the station's fund-raising drive?

   a. $920,000
   b. $137,110
   c. $127,110
   d. $237,110
   e. none of the above

8. Joe bought the window shade at the right. When he got home, he found out that it was $2\frac{3}{8}$ inches too narrow. What size window shade does he need?

   a. $24\frac{3}{8}$ inches

   b. $29\frac{1}{8}$ inches

   c. $28\frac{1}{2}$ inches

   d. 24 inches

   e. none of the above

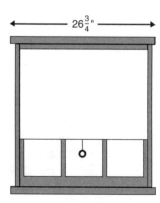

$26\frac{3}{4}$"

9. To heat her house last winter, Mrs. George used $\frac{5}{8}$ cord of wood in February and $\frac{1}{12}$ cord of wood in March. How much wood did she use?

   a. $\frac{3}{10}$ cord

   b. $\frac{13}{24}$ cord

   c. $\frac{1}{2}$ cord

   d. $\frac{3}{4}$ cord

   e. none of the above

10. A gallon of economy paint contained 3.4 tubes of pigment per gallon. The high-quality paint contained 5.15 tubes of pigment per gallon. What was the difference between the amount of pigment used for each paint?

   a. 4.81 tubes

   b. 5.49 tubes

   c. 8.55 tubes

   d. 2.35 tubes

   e. none of the above

11. A radioactive tracer lost $\frac{1}{2}$ of its radioactivity in an hour. Three hours later it had lost another $\frac{7}{16}$ of its radioactivity. What was the total loss in radioactivity for the entire time?

   a. $\frac{7}{32}$ of its radioactivity

   b. $\frac{15}{16}$ of its radioactivity

   c. $\frac{4}{9}$ of its radioactivity

   d. $\frac{1}{16}$ of its radioactivity

   e. none of the above

12. A gypsy moth grew 0.03 gram from the size shown at the right. How much did the gypsy moth weigh after growing?

   a. 2.08 grams

   b. 2.74 grams

   c. 3.10 grams

   d. 2.80 grams

   e. none of the above

Gypsy Moth

2.77 grams

MULTIPLICATION AND DIVISION WORD PROBLEMS: WHOLE NUMBERS

Identifying Multiplication Key Words

In arithmetic, there are four basic operations: addition, subtraction, multiplication, and division. As you have seen, subtraction can be thought of as the opposite of addition. In the same way, division can be thought of as the opposite of multiplication. This concept is useful in deciding whether a problem is a multiplication or a division problem.

In previous chapters, you looked at addition and subtraction key words. There are also multiplication key words.

EXAMPLE 1   Diane always bets $2 on a race. Last night she bet eight times. How much money did she bet?

multiplication key word: times

EXAMPLE 2   It cost Fernando $39 per day to rent a car. He rented a car for 4 days. How much did he pay to rent the car?

multiplication key word: per

> **Remember:** *Per* means "for each."

Multiplication can also be considered repeated addition. Therefore, it is possible for an addition key word to also be a multiplication key word. *Total* is a word that can indicate either addition or multiplication.

In the following problems, circle the multiplication key words. DO NOT SOLVE!

1. Miguel pays his landlord $670 for rent 12 times a year. How much rent does he pay in a year?

2. During the 9 months that she stayed in her apartment, Isabelle paid $43 per month for electricity. How much did she pay for electricity during the time she stayed in her apartment?

3. At the stable, one horse eats 3 pounds of hay a day. What is the total amount of hay needed to feed 26 horses?

4. When her children were young, Alzette had a part-time job for 18 hours a week. She now works twice as many hours as she did then. How many hours a week does she work now?

5. Sam and Marion bought a new home on an 80-by-90 foot lot. How large, in square feet, was the lot?

6. Amy's living room is 24 feet long and 16 feet wide. What is the area of her living room?

7. Sally's research found that every dollar invested in campaign fund-raising was multiplied eight times by new contributions. If her research is correct, how much in new contributions can she expect if she invests $3,600 in fundraising?

8. Fresh orange juice has 14 calories per ounce. How many calories are in an 8-ounce serving of orange juice?

9. Margo's family drinks 3 gallons of milk per week. At $1.75 per gallon, how much does Margo spend each week for milk?

Solving Multiplication Word Problems with Key Words

Look at the following examples of multiplication key words.

EXAMPLE 1 Shirley cleans the kitchen sink three times a week. How many times does she clean the sink in 4 weeks?

> **STEP 1** *question:* How many times does she clean the sink?
>
> **STEP 2** *necessary information:* 3 times a week, 4 weeks
>
> **STEP 3** Decide what arithmetic operation to use.
>
> *multiplication key word:* times
>
> **STEP 4** 3 times a week × 4 weeks = **12 times**

$$\begin{array}{r} 3 \\ \times\ 4 \\ \hline 12 \end{array}$$

EXAMPLE 2 During the Depression, eggs cost 14 cents per dozen. How much did 5 dozen eggs cost?

> **STEP 1** *question:* How much did 5 dozen eggs cost?
>
> **STEP 2** *necessary information:* 14 cents per dozen, 5 dozen
>
> **STEP 3** Decide what arithmetic operation to use.
>
> *multiplication key word:* per
>
> **STEP 4** 14 cents per dozen × 5 = **70 cents**

$$\begin{array}{r} 14 \\ \times\ 5 \\ \hline 70\ cents \end{array}$$

In the problems below, underline the necessary information, and circle the multiplication key words. Then solve the problem.

1. Artificially flavored vanilla ice cream costs 92 cents a pint. All-natural vanilla ice cream costs twice as much. How much does the all-natural ice cream cost?

2. Alan needs to buy 4 sets of guitar strings. There are 6 strings per set. How many strings will he buy?

3. Honest Furniture Company's advertisement plays on the radio five times a day and appears in twelve newspapers. How many times does its ad play on the radio in a week?

4. The We Fix-it Company charges $75 per hour to repair computers. The We Fit-it repairman worked for 3 hours repairing computers at the Long Distance Trucking Company. How much did the Long Distance Trucking Company pay for this work?

Identifying Division Key Words

As you should suspect by now, there are also division key words.

EXAMPLE 1   Ron and Nancy shared equally the cost of a $86 phone bill. How much did each of them pay?

division key words: shared equally, each

> **Remember:** Any word indicating that something is cut up is a division key word.

EXAMPLE 2   The 9 million dollar lottery prize will be divided equally among the 3 winners. How much money will each winner receive?

division key words: divided equally, each

Each is considered a division key word, since it indicates that you are given many things and are looking for one.

Circle the division key words. DO NOT SOLVE!

1. Carlos, Dan, and Juan share the driving equally when they drove from Chicago to Los Angeles. How much did Carlos drive according to the map below?

2,436 miles — Chicago — Los Angeles

2. A bakery produced 6,300 chocolate chip cookies in a day. The cookies were packed in boxes with 36 cookies per box. How many boxes were used that day?

3. Three salesmen sold $2,250 worth of power tools. On the average, how much did each of them sell?

4. It cost $96 to rent the gym for the basketball game. If the 12 players shared the cost equally, how much did each of them pay?

Solving Division Word Problems with Key Words

Knowing the division key words can help you solve division word problems.

EXAMPLE 1 Union dues of $104 a year can be divided into 52 weekly payments. How much is a weekly payment?

STEP 1 *question:* How much is a weekly payment?

STEP 2 *necessary information:* $104 a year, 52 weekly payments

STEP 3 *division key words:* divided

STEP 4 $104 ÷ 52 weekly payments = **$2**

$$52\overline{)104}^{\,2}$$

EXAMPLE 2 A 48-minute basketball game is divided into four equal periods. How long is each period?

STEP 1 *question:* How long is each period?

STEP 2 *necessary information:* 48 minutes, 4 periods

STEP 3 *division key words:* divided, equal, each

STEP 4 48 minutes ÷ 4 periods = **12 minutes**

$$4\overline{)48}^{\,12}$$

For the problems below, underline the necessary information, and circle the division key words. Then solve the word problem.

1. The chocolate bar at the right was shared equally among four children. How much chocolate did each child receive?

12 oz

2. A 60-minute hockey game is divided into three equal periods. How long is the third period?

3. A washing machine that costs $319 when new costs $156 used and can be paid for in 12 monthly payments. How much is each payment on the used washer?

4. A package of 24 mints costs 96 cents. How much does each mint cost?

5. Raffle tickets cost $3 each. If the prizes are worth $4,629, how many tickets must be sold for the raffle to break even?

Key Word Lists for Multiplication and Division

As with addition and subtraction, you can compile lists of multiplication and division key words.

Generally, in multiplication word problems, you are given one of something and asked to find many. You can also think of these problems as multiplying together two parts to get a total.

MULTIPLICATION KEY WORDS

multiplied	as much
times	twice
total	by
of	area
per	volume

Generally, in division word problems, you are given many things and asked to find one. You can also think of these problems as dividing a total by a part to get the other part.

DIVISION KEY WORDS

divided (equally)	average
split	every
each	out of
cut	ratio
equal pieces	shared

Remember: Key words are only a clue for solving a problem. Any key word can also appear in word problems needing the opposite operation in order to be solved. You need to read for understanding.

Mental Math with Multiplication and Division

An important mental math tool is multiplying or dividing by 10, 100, or 1,000. Try to multiply 15 by 10. What is your result?

How about 15×100? $15 \times 1,000$?

$15 \times 10 = 150$. $15 \times 100 = 1,500$. $15 \times 1,000 = 15,000$. Do you see a pattern? Test the pattern with other numbers.

Mental Math: When you multiply by 10, 100, or 1,000, mentally add one, two, or three zeros to the right of the number being multiplied. You can also think of this as moving the decimal point to the right one, two, or three places.

Now try dividing 240 by 10. What is your result?

How about $240 \div 100$? $240 \div 1,000$? What is the pattern? Test this pattern with other numbers.

Mental Math: When you divide by 10, 100, or 1,000, move the decimal point of the number being divided to the left one, two, or three places. If the number ends with zeros, you can also mentally subtract one, two, or three zeros.

When you multiply or divide by 10, 100, or 1,000 throughout this book or in your daily life, use mental math either to add on or take off the correct number of zeros or to move the decimal point the correct number of places.

 Mentally multiply these problems.

1. $55 \times 100 =$ $72.6 \times 1,000 =$ $450 \times 10 =$

2. $43 \times 1,000 =$ $99 \times 100 =$ $700 \times 10 =$

 Mentally divide these problems.

3. $38,000 \div 100 =$ $4,493 \div 10 =$ $772 \div 1,000 =$

4. $480 \div 10 =$ $2,972 \div 100 =$ $1,092 \div 1,000 =$

Solving Multiplication and Division Problems with Key Words

In this exercise, some of the word problems have multiplication key words and some have division key words. In each problem, circle the key words. Identify the circled word as a multiplication or division key word. Then solve the problem.

1. The pizza shown at the right is to be divided equally among four people. How many pieces will each person get?

2. An oil well made a profit of $90,000 last year. How much money will each of the five investors receive if all of the profits are divided equally among them?

3. A gas station owner charges $22 per oil change. In one day he did 15 oil changes. What was the total amount of money he received for oil changes?

4. In the discount store, a dress cost $47. In an expensive downtown store, the same dress cost twice as much. How much did the dress cost at the expensive store?

5. To earn a high school equivalency certificate, a student in Illinois must score 225 points on five tests but no less than 40 points on each test. What is the average score on each test that a student needs to get the certificate?

6. Marge's new car averages 28 miles per gallon of gas. How many miles can she expect to drive after she has filled her 15-gallon tank?

Deciding When to Multiply and When to Divide

Word problems are rarely so simple that you can solve them just by finding key words. You must develop your comprehension of the meaning of word problems. Key words are an aid to that understanding.

In earlier chapters, you learned that the same key word that helped you decide to add in one problem might also appear in a subtraction problem. The same is true with multiplication and division key words.

But Don't Despair!

Learning what the key words mean is the first step to understanding word problems.

In the examples that follow, you are given two numbers and are asked to find a third. In each example, you must decide whether to multiply or divide.

The question will ask you to find a total amount, or it will give you a total amount and ask you to find a part.

- When you are given the parts and asked to find the total, you should multiply.

- When you are given the total and a part and you are asked to find a missing part, you should divide.

To get a better idea of this and of what is meant by *part* and *total,* read the two examples on the next page.

EXAMPLE 1 Each of the city's 24 snowplows can plow 94 miles of road a day. If all snowplows are running, how many miles of road can be plowed by the city plows in one day?

STEP 1 *question:* How many miles of road can be plowed?

STEP 2 *necessary information:* 24 snowplows, 94 miles of road

STEP 3 Decide what arithmetic operation to use. Use the following method to draw a diagram.

Draw two boxes, and label them *part* and *part*.

Put another box above them, and label it *total*.

Fill in the boxes with information from the problem. Use only the information that is needed to solve the problem.

Put 24 in the first *part* box, since that is the number of snowplows. Put 94 in the other *part* box, since that is the number of miles each snowplow can plow.

The box that is empty represents the amount that you are looking for, the total number of miles of road.

Since the box representing the total is empty, you should multiply.

STEP 4 snowplows × miles per snowplow = total miles

24 snowplows × 94 miles = **2,256 miles**

$$
\begin{array}{r}
94 \\
\times\ 24 \\
\hline
376 \\
1\,88 \\
\hline
2{,}256
\end{array}
$$

EXAMPLE 2 A city has 24 snowplows to plow its 2,256 miles of road. How many miles of road must each snowplow cover in order to plow all the city's roads?

STEP 1 *question:* How many miles of road must each snowplow cover?

STEP 2 *necessary information:* 24 snowplows, 2,256 miles of road

STEP 3 Draw and label the boxes.

Put 24 in the first *part* box, since that is the number of snowplows. Put 2,256 in the *total* box, since that has been given as the total number of miles.

The box that is empty represents the amount that you are looking for.

Since the total has been given, you should divide to find the missing part.

STEP 4   total miles ÷ snowplows = miles per snowplow

2,256 miles ÷ 24 snowplows = **94 miles**

$$\begin{array}{r} 94 \\ 24\overline{)2{,}256} \\ \underline{2\ 16} \\ 96 \\ \underline{96} \\ 0 \end{array}$$

Examples 1 and 2 are really discussing the same situation. In the first example, the number of plows and miles for each plow are given; you are asked to find the total number of miles that can be covered, and you should multiply. In the second example, the total number of miles are given as well as the number of plows to be used. In this case, you are looking for a missing part (the miles for each plow) and should divide.

For each problem, draw *part* and *total* boxes. Then solve the problem.

1. A supermarket sold 78 cartons of Dixie cups. There were 50 cups in every carton. How many cups were sold?

2. Juanita spends an average of $16 a day for food for her family. How much did she spend during the 30-day month of June?

3. The *Washington Post*'s morning edition was 140 pages long, and the evening edition was 132 pages long. Of each edition, 780,000 copies were printed. How many pages of newsprint were needed to print the morning edition?

4. Fernando's car gets 18 miles per gallon. How many miles can he drive on 21 gallons of gasoline?

5. In one year, 46,720 people died in car accidents. What was the average number of deaths each day?

6. A factory produces 68,400 nails a day. Every box is packed with 150 nails. How many boxes does the factory need in one day?

Using Diagrams When Deciding to Multiply or Divide

Drawing a picture or diagram is one important strategy for deciding whether to multiply or divide in order to solve a word problem. Look at how a picture or diagram could have helped you solve Example 1 from page 70.

EXAMPLE 1 Each of the city's 24 snowplows can plow 94 miles of road a day. If all snowplows are running, how many miles of road can be plowed by the city plows in one day?

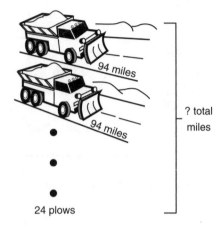

? total miles

94 miles

94 miles

24 plows

STEP 1 *question:* How many miles of road can be plowed?

STEP 2 *necessary information:* 24 snowplows, 94 miles of road

STEP 3 Draw a diagram and decide what arithmetic operation to use.

The diagram shows each of the 24 snowplows plowing 94 miles of road. To find the total miles, you should multiply.

STEP 4 Do the arithmetic.

24 × 94 = **2,256 total miles**

$$\begin{array}{r} 94 \\ \times 24 \\ \hline 376 \\ 188 \\ \hline 2{,}256 \end{array}$$

STEP 5 Make sure the answer is sensible by using estimation.

Over 20 snowplows must each plow nearly 100 miles. An answer near 2,000 miles makes sense.

EXAMPLE 2 A pint of floor wax covers 2,400 square feet of floor. How many pints of floor wax are needed to wax the 168,000-square-foot floor of the airline terminal?

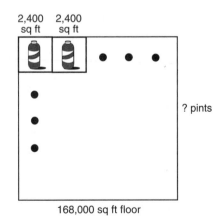

2,400 sq ft   2,400 sq ft

? pints

168,000 sq ft floor

STEP 1 *question:* How many pints of floor wax are needed?

STEP 2 *necessary information:* 1 pint per 2,400 square feet, 168,000 square feet

STEP 3 Draw a diagram and decide what arithmetic operation to use.

The diagram shows that the 168,000-square-foot airline terminal floor must be divided into sections, each 2,400 square feet (the amount covered by one pint of floor wax). To find the number of pints of floor wax, you should divide.

STEP 4   Do the arithmetic.

168,000 ÷ 2,400 = **70 pints of wax**

STEP 5   Make sure the answer is sensible.

You must wax almost 200,000 square feet divided into 2,500 square feet sections. 200,000 ÷ 2,500 = about 80, so 70 pints makes sense.

$$
2,400 \overline{)168,000} \quad 70
$$
$$
\underline{168\,00}
$$
$$
\underline{00}
$$
$$
\underline{00}
$$

....

Each word problem is followed by two diagrams with short explanations. One choice of a diagram and explanation gives you a reason to multiply to find the answer. The other gives you a reason to divide to find the answer. Circle the letter of the correct explanation and solve the problem.

1.   Larry feeds each of his 380 laboratory animals 5 ounces of food pellets a day. How many ounces of food pellets does he need for one day?

a.   Since each animal eats 5 ounces, multiply to find the total ounces needed.

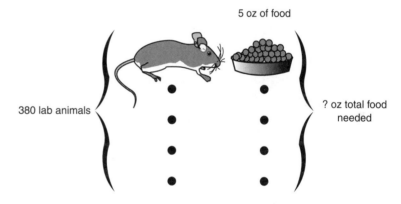

380 lab animals   5 oz of food   ? oz total food needed

b.   To find the amount of food available, divide the total animals (380) by the amount of food available for each.

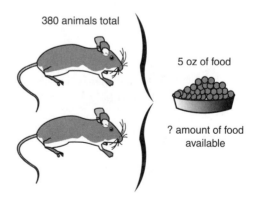

380 animals total   5 oz of food   ? amount of food available

2. Tickets to the play were $6. At the end of the night, Janet counted $3,102 in receipts for the performance. How many people bought tickets for the play?

    a. To find the total $ for people, multiply the cost of a ticket ($6) by the receipts ($3,102).

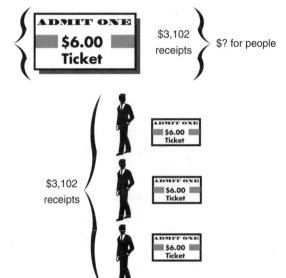

    b. To find the number of people, divide the amount of receipts ($3,102) by the price of one ticket ($6).

3. After filling up her gas tank, Jean drove 260 miles. After the drive, she refilled her tank with 13 gallons of gas. On the average, how many miles was she able to drive on a gallon of gas?

    a. To find the total miles, multiply the miles for a car (260) by the gallons (13).

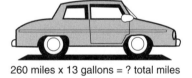

260 miles x 13 gallons = ? total miles

    b. To find the miles per gallon, divide the miles (260) by the number of gallons (13).

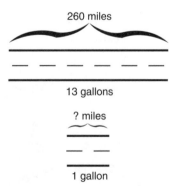

260 miles

13 gallons

? miles

1 gallon

4. Glennie planted 8 rows of tomatoes in her truck garden. If she planted 48 plants in each row, how many tomato plants did she plant?

   a. Since there are 8 rows and 48 plants in each row, you should multiply.

   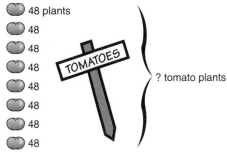

   b. To find the number of plants, divide 48 plants by 8 rows.

5. Shirley, a buyer for a major department store, has a budget of $6,000 to buy 400 blouses. What is the most she can pay per blouse?

   a. To find the most Shirley can pay for one blouse, divide the total budget ($6,000) by the number of blouses (400).

   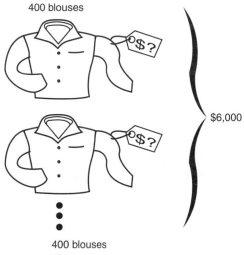

   b. To find the total paid, multiply the budget ($6,000) by the number of blouses (400).

Underline the correct phrase by using the solution given after each word problem. The first one is done for you.

6. A football television contract for $78,000,000 is to be _____ 60 colleges. How much will each college receive?

$$\frac{\$\ 1,300,000}{60\ \text{colleges} \overline{)\$78,000,000}}\ (\underline{\text{divided equally among}},\ \text{given to each of})$$

7. Mary bought 4 skirts for $24 _____. How much did she spend?

$$\begin{array}{r} \$24 \\ \times\ 4\ \text{skirts} \\ \hline \$96 \end{array} \quad (\text{total, each})$$

8. There were 36,000 trees _____ in the state forest before the fire. During the fire, 48 square miles of forest burned. How many trees were destroyed in all?

$$\begin{array}{r} 36,000\ \text{trees} \\ \times\ \quad 48\ \text{square miles} \\ \hline 1,728,000\ \text{trees} \end{array} \quad (\text{total, per square mile})$$

9. During an average 12-hour workday, the fast-food restaurant sold 3,852 hamburgers.

$$\frac{\textbf{321 hamburgers}}{12\ \text{hours} \overline{)3,852\ \text{hamburgers}}}$$ (How hamburgers were sold in a week?, How many hamburgers were sold per hour?)

10. A cafeteria serves 3,820 _____ a day, with each person being served an 8-ounce portion of soup. How many ounces of soup must be made in one day?

$$\begin{array}{r} 3,820 \\ \times\ \quad 8\ \text{oz of soup} \\ \hline \textbf{30,560 oz of soup} \end{array} \quad (\text{ounces of soup, people})$$

MULTIPLICATION AND DIVISION WORD PROBLEMS: DECIMALS AND FRACTIONS

Solving Decimal Multiplication and Division Word Problems

Fraction and decimal word problems are solved in the same ways as word problems using whole numbers.

The following examples show a method for solving multiplication and division word problems containing decimals. As with whole-number word problems, multiply when you are looking for the total, and divide when you are looking for one of the parts. Estimation can be very helpful with these problems.

EXAMPLE 1 Gasoline costs $1.499 per gallon. How much do 18 gallons of gasoline cost?

STEP 1 *question:* How much do 18 gallons of gasoline cost?

STEP 2 *necessary information:* $1.499 per gallon, 18 gallons

STEP 3 *diagram:*

```
        ?
      total

    18    1.499
   part    part
```

STEP 4 price of each gallon × number of gallons = total cost

$18 \times \$1.499 = 26.982 =$ **$26.98**

(In money problems that have answers containing more than two decimal places, you should round your answer to the nearest cent.)

$$\begin{array}{r} 1.499 \\ \times18 \\ \hline 11992 \\ 1499 \\ \hline 26.982 \end{array}$$

STEP 5 *estimation:* $18 \times 1.5 = 27$

This estimation shows that the answer is sensible.

EXAMPLE 2 Gil's car gets 28.6 miles per gallon. Last month he drove 943.8 miles. How many gallons of gas did he need for the month?

STEP 1 *question:* How many gallons of gas did he need for the month?

STEP 2 *necessary information:* 28.6 miles per gallon, 943.8 miles

STEP 3 *diagram:*

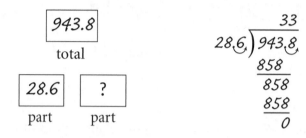

943.8
total

28.6	?
part	part

STEP 4 total miles ÷ miles per gallon = gallons

943.8 miles ÷ 28.6 miles per gallon = **33 gallons**

STEP 5 *estimation:* 900 ÷ 30 = 30

Calculator: Your calculator can be very useful when multiplying or dividing decimals. But you must be careful about putting the decimal in the correct place. It is important that you estimate the answer to your problem before doing the calculator work, so you will know that you entered the numbers correctly on the calculator.

If you made a mistake entering the decimal point and got a result of 3.3 gallons, your estimate should alert you.

For each problem, use *part* and *total* boxes to help you decide whether to multiply or divide. Then solve the problem. Remember to write the label of the answer and to round all money problems to the nearest cent.

1. A runner ran an average of 6.5 minutes per mile for a race that had 242 official entrants. If the race was 6.2 miles long, how long did it take him or her to run it?

total

part	part

2. A nonprofit food co-op bought a 40-pound sack of onions for $23.20. How much will the co-op members pay per pound if the onions are sold at cost?

total

part	part

3. After filling her gas tank, Katie drove 159.75 miles. After the ride, she filled her tank again with 7.1 gallons of gas. On the average, how many miles per gallon did she get on the trip?

total

part   part

4. A beef round roast costs $2.29 per pound. How much is a 4.67-pound roast?

total

part   part

5. Four roommates share their food bill equally. Last month they spent $372.36 for food and $850.00 for rent. How much did each of them pay for food?

total

part   part

6. A salesman, working on commission, earned $118.56 in an 8-hour workday. On the average, how much did he earn each hour?

total

part   part

7. It costs $0.85 to ride the city bus. At the end of the day, Veronique emptied the bus's cash box and deposited $167.45 in fares. How many passengers rode the bus that day?

total

part   part

8. Lynelle spent $3.65 for transportation every work day. Last year she worked 239 days. How much did she spend on transportation during work days last year?

total

part   part

Solving Fraction Multiplication Word Problems

When you multiply two whole numbers, the answer is larger than either number. But when you multiply a number by a fraction smaller than 1, the answer is smaller than the original number. For example, $21 \times \frac{2}{3} = 14$.

Multiplication and division word problems with fractions often seem confusing. When you multiply by a fraction, you may end up with a smaller number, and when you divide by a fraction, you may end up with a larger number. This is the opposite of what you have come to expect with whole numbers.

The following chart should help you remember when to expect a larger or smaller answer when multiplying or dividing.

When Multiplying a Number By:	Your Answer Will Be:	Example:
a number greater than 1	larger than the number	$36 \times 2 = 72$
1	the same as the number	$36 \times 1 = 36$
a fraction smaller than 1	smaller than the number	$\overset{9}{36} \times \frac{3}{\underset{1}{4}} = 27$
(**Remember:** *An improper fraction is greater than 1. For example,* $36 \times \frac{4}{3} = 48$.)		

When Dividing a Number By:	Your Answer Will Be:	Example:
a number greater than 1	smaller than the number	$36 \div 2 = \overset{18}{36} \times \frac{1}{\underset{1}{2}} = 18$
1	the same as the number	$36 \div 1 = 36$
a fraction smaller than 1	larger than the number	$36 \div \frac{3}{4} = \overset{12}{36} \times \frac{4}{\underset{1}{3}} = 48$
(*Dividing by an improper fraction is the same as multiplying by a fraction less than 1. For example,* $36 \div \frac{4}{3} = \overset{9}{36} \times \frac{3}{\underset{1}{4}} = 27$.)		

The most common key word in fraction multiplication problems is *of*—as in *finding a fraction of* something. Some people confuse these problems with division because they require you to find a piece of something. The example below illustrates why you multiply when you find a fraction of a quantity.

Find $\frac{1}{2}$ of 6.

You already know that this is 3. Multiplying by $\frac{1}{2}$ gives the same result as dividing by 2. When you multiply the two numbers, you really multiply the numerators (the numbers above the line) and divide by the denominator (the number below the line).

$$\frac{1}{2} \times 6 = \frac{1}{_1\cancel{2}} \times \frac{\cancel{6}^3}{1} = \frac{3}{1} = 3$$

The following examples show you how to solve multiplication word problems that require you to find a fraction of a quantity.

EXAMPLE 1   Bernie's Service Station inspected 20 cars yesterday. Of the 20 cars inspected, $\frac{1}{5}$ failed the inspection. How many cars failed the inspection?

> **STEP 1**   *question:* How many cars failed the inspection?
>
> **STEP 2**   *necessary information:* 20 cars, $\frac{1}{5}$ of the cars
>
> **STEP 3**   *key word:* of
>
> fraction (of) × total = part
>
> **STEP 4** $\frac{1}{5} \times 20$ cars = cars that failed
>
> $\frac{1}{_1\cancel{5}} \times \frac{\cancel{20}^4}{1} =$ **4 cars**

Some multiplication word problems that involve fractions do not have the key word *of.* These problems can be recognized as multiplication, since you are usually given the size of one item and asked to find the size of many. To go from one to many, you should multiply.

EXAMPLE 2   In a high school, class periods are $\frac{3}{4}$ hour long. How long will 8 periods last?

> **STEP 1**   *question:* How long will 8 periods last?
>
> **STEP 2**   *necessary information:* $\frac{3}{4}$ hour, 8 periods
>
> **STEP 3**   You are given the length of one class period ($\frac{3}{4}$ hour) and are asked to find the total length of many class periods (8 periods). Therefore, you should multiply.
>
> **STEP 4**   8 periods × $\frac{3}{4}$ hour $= \frac{^2\cancel{8} \times \frac{3}{\cancel{4}_1} =$ **6 hours**

When you are working with a word problem and have to decide whether to multiply or divide, it is especially helpful to use **Step 5: Check to see that your answer is sensible.**

In Example 2, if you had mistakenly divided 8 by $\frac{3}{4}$, your answer would have been $10\frac{2}{3}$ hours. ($8 \div \frac{3}{4} = 8 \times \frac{4}{3} = 10\frac{2}{3}$.) Would it make sense to say that 8 periods, each consisting of less than 1 hour, would total $10\frac{2}{3}$ hours?

In the following problems, underline the necessary information. Then solve the problem.

1. In Chicago last year $\frac{2}{3}$ of the precipitation was rain. According to the chart, how many inches of rain fell in Chicago?

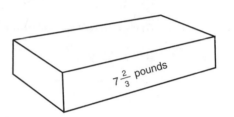

Precipitation	
Baltimore	27 inches
Chicago	36 inches
New York	40 inches

2. Of the car accidents in the state last year, $\frac{7}{8}$ were in urban areas. There were 23,352 car accidents in the state last year. How many accidents were in urban areas?

3. How much do 10 of the boxes shown at the right weigh?

$7\frac{2}{3}$ pounds

4. Brad's dog Cedar eats $\frac{2}{3}$ can of dog food and two dog biscuits a day. How many cans of dog food will Brad need to feed Cedar for 12 days?

5. A candy bar contains $1\frac{1}{8}$ ounces of peanuts. How many ounces of peanuts are in $3\frac{1}{2}$ candy bars?

6. Only $\frac{1}{2}$ cup of a new concentrated liquid detergent is needed to clean a full load of laundry. How much detergent is needed to clean $\frac{1}{2}$ of a load of laundry?

7. In a $\frac{1}{4}$-pound hamburger, $\frac{2}{5}$ of the hamburger meat was fat. How much fat was in the hamburger?

8. A space shuttle was traveling 17,000 miles per hour. How far did it travel in $2\frac{1}{2}$ hours?

Solving Fraction Division Word Problems

Remember that the second number in a fraction division problem will be inverted (turned upside down). Therefore, it is very important that the total amount that is being divided is always the first number that you write when solving such a problem. But even though the total amount comes first when you are solving the fraction division problem, it does not always appear first in a word problem.

EXAMPLE 1 Joyce made dinner for nine people. She divided a $\frac{1}{4}$-pound stick of butter equally among them. How much butter did each person receive?

> STEP 1 *question:* How much butter did each person receive?
>
> STEP 2 *necessary information:* $\frac{1}{4}$ pound, 9 people
>
> STEP 3 *key words:* divided equally, each
>
> Nine people are sharing the butter. To find how much butter one person receives, you should divide.
>
> STEP 4 total butter ÷ number of people = butter per person
>
> $\frac{1}{4}$ pound ÷ 9 people = $\frac{1}{4} \times \frac{1}{9} = \frac{1}{36}$ **pound per person**

> **Remember:** The total amount is not always the largest number.

Many division word problems contain the concept of cutting a total into pieces. If you are given the size of the total, you should divide to find a part—either the number of pieces or the size of each piece.

EXAMPLE 2 Quality Butter Company makes butter in 60-pound batches. It then cuts each batch into $\frac{1}{4}$-pound sticks of butter. How many sticks of butter are made from each batch?

> STEP 1 *question:* How many sticks of butter are made from each batch?
>
> STEP 2 *necessary information:* 60-lb batches, $\frac{1}{4}$-lb sticks
>
> STEP 3 *key words:* cuts, each
>
> total amount ÷ size of each piece = number of pieces
>
> STEP 4 60-pound batches ÷ $\frac{1}{4}$-pound sticks = $\frac{60}{1} \div \frac{1}{4} =$
> $\frac{60}{1} \times \frac{4}{1} = 60 \times 4 =$ **240 sticks**

Underline the necessary information in each problem below. Then solve the problem.

1. A box of $22\frac{1}{2}$ inches deep. How many books can be packed in the box if each book is $\frac{5}{8}$ inch thick?

2. Gloria is serving a dinner for 13 people. She is cooking a $6\frac{1}{2}$-pound roast. How much meat would each person get if she divided the roast equally?

3. A bookstore gift wraps books using $2\frac{1}{4}$ feet of ribbon for each book. How many books can the store gift wrap from a roll of ribbon $265\frac{1}{2}$ feet long?

4. A container contains $8\frac{1}{2}$ pounds of mashed potatoes. Linh, who works in a cafeteria, divide the potatoes into servings the size shown at the right. How many servings can she make from the container of potatoes?

Mashed Potatoes

$\frac{1}{2}$ pound

5. A can of Diet Delight peaches contains $9\frac{3}{4}$ ounces of peaches. If one can is used for three equal servings, how large would each serving be?

6. Tatiana wants to divide the garden shown at the right into $1\frac{1}{2}$-foot-wide sections. How many sections can she make?

12 feet

Solving Fraction Multiplication and Division Word Problems

Underline the necessary information and decide whether to multiply or divide. Then solve the problem.

1. A music practice room is used 12 hours a day. If each practice session is $\frac{3}{4}$ hour long, how many sessions are there in a day?

2. At full production, a car rolls off the assembly line every $\frac{2}{3}$ hour. At this rate, how long does it take to produce 30 cars?

3. At full production, a car rolls off the assembly line every $\frac{2}{3}$ hour. At this rate, how many cars are produced in 24 hours?

4. A consumer group claimed that $\frac{2}{3}$ of all microwave ovens were defective. The chart shows oven sales in one state last year. According to the consumer group's findings, how many microwave ovens sold in this state would have been defective?

Oven Sales	
Microwave	26,148
Regular	59,882

5. On a wilderness hike, six hikers had to share $4\frac{1}{2}$ pounds of chocolate bar and $1\frac{3}{4}$ pounds of dry milk. If it was cut equally, how much chocolate did each hiker receive?

6. A recipe calls for the ingredients at the right. If a cook wants to double the recipe, how much baking soda will he or she need?

1 tsp baking powder

$1\frac{1}{2}$ tsp baking soda

$\frac{1}{2}$ tsp salt

Put a check next to the correct question to complete each problem below. Use the solution given after each word problem.

7. For her printer, Awilda bought a toner cartridge that contained 3.5 ounces of toner. The toner is supposed to last for 5,000 copies.
(_____ On the average, how many copies can be made per ounce of toner?)
(_____ On the average, how much toner is used for each copy?)

$$\begin{array}{r} 0.0007 \\ 5{,}000\overline{)3.5000} \end{array}$$

8. Elena used to pay $0.13 a minute to call her mother long distance. Since she changed to her new phone company, she now pays $0.09 a minute. This month she talked to her mother for 56 minutes.
(_____ What will the new phone company charge for her talks with her mother?)
(_____ What would her old phone company charge for her talks with her mother?)

$$\begin{array}{r} \$0.09 \\ \times\ \ 56 \\ \hline \$5.04 \end{array}$$

9. In order to cut down the amount of fat in her family's diet, Alejandrina decided to use only $\frac{2}{3}$ of the butter called for in a recipe. Her recipe for brownies originally called for $\frac{1}{2}$ cup of butter.
(_____ How much butter should she use if she wanted to double the brownie recipe?)
(_____ How much butter should she use for her new brownie recipe?)

$\frac{1}{2} \times \frac{2}{3} = \frac{1}{3}$ cup

10. A package of 30 fig bars weighs 16 ounces.
(_____ What is the total weight of 16 packages of fig bars?)
(_____ How much does a single fig bar weigh?)

$$\begin{array}{r} 0.53\ \ \ \text{or } 5\frac{1}{3}\text{ oz} \\ 30\overline{)16.0000} \\ \underline{150}\ \ \ \ \ \ \ \\ 100\ \ \ \ \\ \underline{90}\ \ \ \\ 100 \end{array}$$

Solving Multiplication and Division Word Problems

For each problem, circle the letter of the correct answer. Round money problems to the nearest cent and other decimal problems to the nearest hundredth.

1. Forty pounds of mayonnaise were packed in jars that weighed $\frac{1}{8}$ pound and could hold $\frac{5}{8}$ pound of mayonnaise. How many jars were needed to pack all the mayonnaise?

   a. 25 jars
   b. 64 jars
   c. 41 jars
   d. 320 jars
   e. 5 jars

2. A 32-square-foot piece of $\frac{1}{4}$-inch-thick plywood costs $20.80. How much does it cost per square foot?

   a. $52.80
   b. $11.20
   c. $0.65
   d. $12.80
   e. $5.20

3. To cover the cost of the prizes, a VFW Post had to sell at least $\frac{1}{6}$ of the raffle tickets. They had 3,000 raffle tickets printed. How many tickets did they have to sell?

   a. 5,000 raffle tickets
   b. 500 raffle tickets
   c. 1,800 raffle tickets
   d. 18,000 raffle tickets
   e. none of the above

4. The trainer of the championship baseball team was voted $\frac{3}{5}$ of a winner's share. If a winner's share is $17,490 and there were 40 shares, how much money did the trainer receive?

   a. $29,155
   b. $10,494
   c. $437.25
   d. $3,498
   e. $728.75

5. To make one apron, Janice needed $\frac{2}{3}$ yard of cloth. She has a roll of cloth $7\frac{1}{3}$ yards long. If she doesn't waste any cloth, how many aprons can she make by cutting and using the entire roll of cloth?

    a. $4\frac{8}{9}$ aprons
    b. 4 aprons
    c. 5 aprons
    d. 11 aprons
    e. 8 aprons

6. Max used 8.1 gallons of gas when he drove 263.1 miles in 4.5 hours. What was his average speed for the trip? (Round to the nearest tenth.)

    a. 31.1 miles per hour
    b. 58.3 miles per hour
    c. 58.4 miles per hour
    d. 58.5 miles per hour
    e. 31.2 miles per hour

7. The Motown Music Company shipped 1,410 CDs to the Midtown Music Store. If 30 CDs were packed in each box, how many boxes were needed to ship the CDs?

    a. 423 boxes
    b. 470 boxes
    c. 47 boxes
    d. 43 boxes
    e. none of the above

8. Ingrid ran in a race from Templeton to Redfield. One kilometer is equal to 0.62 mile. How many miles did she run?

    a. 24 miles
    b. 9.3 miles
    c. 24.19 miles
    d. 4.13 miles
    e. none of the above

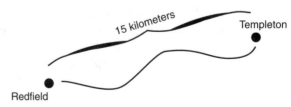

USING PROPORTIONS

What Are Ratios?

A **ratio** is a comparison of two groups. Ratios can be written in a number of ways.

EXAMPLE   A small luncheonette has 8 chairs for 2 tables. The ratio of chairs to tables can be written three ways.

8 chairs for 2 tables

8 to 2, more commonly written as 8:2

$\dfrac{8 \text{ chairs}}{2 \text{ tables}}$

In the rest of this book, you will use only the third way of writing a ratio, the fraction form.

Note: Always write labels for both the top and the bottom of the ratio.

Write the following relationships as ratios in the fraction form. The first problem has been done for you.

1. 1 customer bought 6 cans of tomato soup. $\dfrac{1 \text{ customer}}{6 \text{ cans}}$

2. 2 teachers worked with 30 students.

3. Phi Hung earned 120 dollars in 8 hours.

4. Yvette drove 38 miles on 2 gallons of gasoline.

5. The company provided 3 buses for 114 commuters.

What Are Proportions?

A **proportion** expresses two ratios that have the same value. In arithmetic, you have studied these as equivalent fractions. For example, $\frac{75}{100} = \frac{3}{4}$.

EXAMPLE 1 The center of the city has 1 bus stop every 3 blocks. Therefore, the city center has 2 bus stops every 6 blocks.

$$\frac{1 \text{ bus stop}}{3 \text{ blocks}} = \frac{2 \text{ bus stops}}{6 \text{ blocks}}$$

EXAMPLE 2 The ratio of women to men working at the Small Motors Repair Shop is 3 women to 4 men. If there are 8 men working at the repair shop, how many women work there?

One of the numbers of the proportion is not given: the number of women working at the repair shop. Therefore, when the proportion is written, a placeholder is needed in the place where the number of women should be written. The letter *n*, standing for a number, is used as the placeholder, but any letter could be used.

$$\frac{3 \text{ women}}{4 \text{ men}} = \frac{n \text{ women}}{8 \text{ men}}$$

Finding the number that belongs in place of the *n* is called **solving a proportion.** Look at two methods that can be used to solve a proportion.

Method 1: Multiplication

STEP 1 *question:* How many women work there?

STEP 2 *necessary information:* 3 women, 4 men, 8 men

STEP 3 Write a proportion based on the problem.

$$\frac{3 \text{ women}}{4 \text{ men}} = \frac{n \text{ women}}{8 \text{ men}}$$

$$\frac{3 \times \square}{4 \times \boxed{2}} = \frac{n}{8}$$

Notice that both denominators have been filled in and that $4 \times 2 = 8$.

$$\frac{3 \times \boxed{2}}{4 \times \boxed{2}} = \frac{6}{8}$$

Since proportions are equivalent fractions, you multiply the top and the bottom by the same number. In this problem, the number is 2.

STEP 4 Therefore, $3 \times 2 = $ **6 women.**

There are cases when Method 1 does not work as simply. This is especially true when a problem contains a decimal or a fraction, or when the numbers are not simple multiples of each other. In these problems, Method 2 is quite useful.

Method 2: Cross Multiplication

STEP 1 *question:* How many women work there?

STEP 2 *necessary information:* 3 women, 4 men, 8 men

STEP 3 Write the proportion.

$$\frac{3 \text{ women}}{4 \text{ men}} = \frac{n \text{ women}}{8 \text{ men}}$$

$$\frac{3}{4} \diagup\!\!\!\!\diagdown \frac{n}{8}$$

STEP 4 Cross multiply. Multiply the numbers that are on a diagonal.

$$4 \times n = 3 \times 8$$
$$4n = 24$$

> **Note:** The letter is usually written on the left side. Also, *4n* means the same as 4 times *n*. It is not necessary to write the multiplication sign, ×.

STEP 5 To find *n*, the number of women, divide the number standing alone by the number next to the letter.

$$n = \frac{24}{4} = 6$$

$n =$ **6 women**

Notice that when you write a proportion, the labels must be consistent. For example, if *women* is the label of the top of one side of a proportion, it must be on the top of the other side.

EXAMPLE 3 Chin has seen 6 movies in the last 9 months. At this rate, how many movies will she see in 12 months?

STEP 1 *question:* How many movies will she see in 12 months?

STEP 2 *necessary information:* 6 movies, 9 months, 12 months

STEP 3 Write the proportion.

$$\frac{12 \text{ months}}{n \text{ movies}} = \frac{9 \text{ months}}{6 \text{ movies}}$$

$$\frac{12}{n} \diagup\!\!\!\!\diagdown \frac{9}{6}$$

STEP 4 Cross multiply.

$$9 \times n = 12 \times 6$$
$$9n = 72$$

STEP 5 Divide.

$$n = \frac{72}{9} = 8$$

$n =$ **8 movies**

EXAMPLE 4 Sandy read that she should cook a roast 20 minutes for each half pound. How large a roast could she cook in 90 minutes?

STEP 1 *question:* How large a roast could she cook in 90 minutes?

STEP 2 *necessary information:* $\frac{1}{2}$ pound, 20 minutes, 90 minutes

STEP 3 Write the proportion.

$$\frac{\frac{1}{2} \text{ pound}}{20 \text{ minutes}} = \frac{n \text{ pounds}}{90 \text{ minutes}}$$

$$\frac{\frac{1}{2}}{20} \diagdown \frac{n}{90}$$

STEP 4 Cross multiply.

$$20 \times n = 90 \times \frac{1}{2}$$

STEP 5 Divide.

$$20n = 45$$

$$n = 2\frac{1}{4} \text{ pounds of roast}$$

$$n = \frac{45}{20} = 2\frac{1}{4}$$

Solve the following proportions for *n*.

1. $\dfrac{160 \text{ miles}}{5 \text{ hours}} = \dfrac{n \text{ miles}}{10 \text{ hours}}$

2. $\dfrac{12 \text{ cars}}{32 \text{ people}} = \dfrac{3 \text{ cars}}{n \text{ people}}$

3. $\dfrac{n \text{ dollars}}{8 \text{ quarters}} = \dfrac{6 \text{ dollars}}{24 \text{ quarters}}$

4. $\dfrac{42 \text{ pounds}}{n \text{ chickens}} = \dfrac{14 \text{ pounds}}{4 \text{ chickens}}$

5. $\dfrac{28,928 \text{ people}}{8 \text{ doctors}} = \dfrac{n \text{ people}}{1 \text{ doctor}}$

6. $\dfrac{\$24.39}{1 \text{ shirt}} = \dfrac{n \text{ dollars}}{6 \text{ shirts}}$

7. $\dfrac{\$47.85}{3 \text{ shirts}} = \dfrac{n \text{ dollars}}{10 \text{ shirts}}$

8. $\dfrac{3 \text{ minutes}}{\frac{1}{2} \text{ mile}} = \dfrac{n \text{ minutes}}{5 \text{ miles}}$

9. $\dfrac{575 \text{ passengers}}{n \text{ days}} = \dfrac{1,725 \text{ passengers}}{21 \text{ days}}$

10. $\dfrac{7 \text{ blinks}}{\frac{1}{10} \text{ minute}} = \dfrac{n \text{ blinks}}{10 \text{ minutes}}$

Using Proportions to Solve Word Problems

Proportions can be used when you are unsure of whether to multiply or divide.

The following examples show how to write proportions to solve multiplication and division word problems.

EXAMPLE 1 There are 16 cups in a gallon. At the church picnic, Carmella poured 5 gallons of cola into paper cups that each held 1 cup of soda. How many cups did she fill?

STEP 1 *question:* How many cups did she fill?

STEP 2 *necessary information:* 16 cups in a gallon, 5 gallons, 1 cup

STEP 3 Write the proportion.

labels for proportion: $\dfrac{\text{cups}}{\text{gallons}}$

$$\frac{16 \text{ cups}}{1 \text{ gallon}} = \frac{n \text{ cups}}{5 \text{ gallons}}$$

$$\frac{16}{1} \diagup\!\!\!\!\diagdown \frac{n}{5}$$

STEP 4 Cross multiply.

(*n* means the same as $1 \times n$. From now on you don't need to write the 1 and the $\times$ sign, so you write $n = 16 \times 5$.)

$$n = 16 \times 5$$
$$n = 80$$

$n =$ **80 cups**

Remember: When you write the labels for a proportion, it doesn't matter which category goes on top. But once you make a decision, you must stick with it. Once you put *cups* on the top of one ratio, you must keep *cups* on top of the other.

---

16 cups in a gallon means the same as $\dfrac{16 \text{ cups}}{1 \text{ gallon}}$. The 1 will often not appear in these word problems. When writing a proportion, you must determine when a 1 is needed and where it goes. You can do this by first identifying the two labels and then putting numbers in the proportion.

There are a number of word phrases that require that a 1 be used in a ratio.

Phrases	Meaning
27 miles per gallon	$\dfrac{27 \text{ miles}}{1 \text{ gallon}}$
$8 an hour	$\dfrac{\$8}{1 \text{ hour}}$
3 meals a day	$\dfrac{3 \text{ meals}}{1 \text{ day}}$
30 miles each day	$\dfrac{30 \text{ miles}}{1 \text{ day}}$

EXAMPLE 2 At the Boardwalk Arcade, owner Manuel Santos collects 1,380 quarters every day. There are 4 quarters in a dollar. How many dollars does he collect every day?

STEP 1 *question:* How many dollars does he collect every day?

STEP 2 *necessary information:* 1,380 quarters, 4 quarters in a dollar

STEP 3 *labels for proportion:* $\dfrac{\text{dollars}}{\text{quarters}}$

$$\frac{n \text{ dollars}}{1,380 \text{ quarters}} = \frac{1 \text{ dollar}}{4 \text{ quarter}}$$

$$\frac{n}{1,380} \diagup\hspace{-1.1em}\diagdown \frac{1}{4}$$

STEP 4 Cross multiply.

$$4 \times n = 1,380 \times 1$$
$$4n = 1,380$$

STEP 5 Divide.

$$n = \frac{1,380}{4} = 345$$

$n =$ **345 dollars**

Underline the necessary information. Write proportions for the problems below and solve them.

1. A shipment of vaccine can protect 7,800 people. How many shipments of vaccine are needed to protect 140,400 people living in the Portland area?

2. It costs $340 an hour to run the 1,000-watt power generator. How much does it cost to run the generator for 24 hours?

3. How many ounces of soup (like the can shown at the right) are in a carton containing 28 cans?

4. Jim types 52 words per minute. How many words can he type in 26 minutes?

5. An elementary school nurse used 3,960 Band-Aids last year. There were 180 school days. On the average, how many Band-Aids did he use a day?

6. The company health clinic gave out 5,460 aspirin and 720 antacid tablets last year. How many bottles of aspirin did the clinic use last year if there were 260 aspirin in a bottle?

7. A coal mine produced 126 tons of slag in a week. Trucks removed the slag in 3-ton loads. How many loads were needed to remove all the slag?

8. Cloth is sold by the yard. Edyth bought the piece of cloth shown at the right to make dresses. There are 3 feet in a yard. How many yards of cloth did she buy?

9. A 6-ounce can of water chestnuts contains 26 water chestnuts. Hong used 3 cans of water chestnuts. How many water chestnuts did she use?

Using Proportions to Solve Decimal Word Problems

You can use proportions to solve decimal multiplication and division word problems. The problems should be set up as if the numbers were whole numbers. Multiply or divide as if you were using whole numbers. Then use the rules for decimal multiplication and division to place the decimal point in the right place. Finally, round the answer if necessary.

EXAMPLE 1 Ray has $15.00 to spend on gasoline. How many gallons can he buy if 1 gallon costs $1.20?

STEP 1 *question:* How many gallons can he buy?

STEP 2 *necessary information:* $15.00, $1.20 for a gallon

STEP 3 *labels for proportion:* $\dfrac{\$}{\text{gallons}}$

$$\frac{\$15.00}{n \text{ gallons}} = \frac{\$1.20}{1 \text{ gallon}}$$

STEP 4 Cross multiply.

STEP 5 Divide.

$n =$ **12.5 gallons**

$$\frac{15}{n} \diagdown \frac{1.20}{1}$$

$$1.20 \times n = 15 \times 1$$
$$1.20n = 15$$

$$n = \frac{15}{1.20} = 12.5$$

EXAMPLE 2 There are 236.5 milliliters in a cup. A recipe calls for 3 cups of flour. Maria has only metric spoons and measuring cups. How many milliliters of flour does she need for the recipe?

STEP 1 *question:* How many milliliters of flour does she need for the recipe?

STEP 2 *necessary information:* 236.5 milliliters in a cup, 3 cups

STEP 3 *labels for proportion:* $\dfrac{\text{milliliters}}{\text{cups}}$

$$\frac{236.5 \text{ milliliters}}{1 \text{ cup}} = \frac{n \text{ milliliters}}{3 \text{ cups}}$$

STEP 4 Cross multiply.

$n =$ **709.5 milliliters**

$$\frac{236.5}{1} \diagdown \frac{n}{3}$$

$$n = 3 \times 236.5$$
$$n = 709.5$$

Underline the necessary information. Write the labels for the proportion, fill in the numbers, and solve the proportion. Round your answers to the nearest hundredth.

1. There are 25.4 millimeters in an inch. How many inches long is a 100-millimeter cigarette?

2. A kilogram weight is shown at the right. The police seized 36 kilograms of illegal drugs. How many pounds did the drugs weigh?

3. Alba worked 35.5 hours last week. She earns $8.62 an hour. How much money did she earn last week?

4. There are 1.09 yards in a meter. Gary ran in an 880-yard race. How many meters did he run?

5. Cindy spent $20.00 on gasoline. The gasoline cost $1.15 per gallon. How many gallons of gasoline did she buy?

6. There are approximately 1.61 kilometers in a mile. The speedometer on Iris's imported car is in kilometers per hour. She does not want to speed. What is 55 miles per hour in kilometers per hour?

7. A Tiger Milk nutrition bar weighs 35.4 grams. The factory processed 9,486 bars in one run. How many grams of Tiger Milk bars were processed?

Using Proportions to Solve Fraction Word Problems

Proportions can be used to solve multiplication and division word problems containing fractions. Though they look complicated when you set them up, they are manageable after you cross multiply.

EXAMPLE 1 A dump truck can carry a load of $2\frac{3}{4}$ tons of gravel. In one day, the truck removed 8 loads of gravel from a gravel pit. How many tons of gravel did it remove from the pit that day?

STEP 1 *question:* How many tons of gravel did it remove from the pit that day?

STEP 2 *necessary information:* a load of $2\frac{3}{4}$ tons, 8 loads

STEP 3 *labels for proportion:* $\dfrac{\text{tons}}{\text{loads}}$

$$\frac{2\frac{3}{4}\ \text{tons}}{1\ \text{load}} = \frac{n\ \text{tons}}{8\ \text{loads}}$$

STEP 4 Cross multiply.

$n = $ **22 tons**

$$\frac{2\frac{3}{4}}{1} \diagdown\!\!\!\!\diagup \frac{n}{8}$$

$$n = 8 \times 2\frac{3}{4}$$

$$n = \frac{\overset{2}{\cancel{8}}}{1} \times \frac{11}{\cancel{4}_1} = 22$$

EXAMPLE 2 Top Burger makes a $\frac{1}{4}$-pound hamburger. How many of these hamburgers can be made from 50 pounds of hamburger meat?

STEP 1 *question:* How many of these hamburgers can be made?

STEP 2 *necessary information:* $\frac{1}{4}$ pound, 50 pounds

STEP 3 *labels for proportion:* $\dfrac{\text{pounds}}{\text{hamburgers}}$

$$\frac{\frac{1}{4}\ \text{pound}}{1\ \text{hamburger}} = \frac{50\ \text{pounds}}{n\ \text{hamburgers}}$$

STEP 4 Cross multiply.

STEP 5 Multiply both sides by 4 to clear the n.

$n = $ **200 hamburgers**

$$\frac{\frac{1}{4}}{1} \diagdown\!\!\!\!\diagup \frac{50}{n}$$

$$\tfrac{1}{4} \times n = 50 \times 1$$

$$\tfrac{1}{4}n = 50$$

$$n = 50 \times 4 = 200$$

A word problem asking you to find a fraction of something is easier to solve by direct multiplication than by using a proportion. Example 3 illustrates this.

EXAMPLE 3 Of all gallons of milk sold in a store, $\frac{2}{5}$ are low fat. The store sold 380 gallons of milk. How many gallons of low-fat milk were sold?

You could set up the following proportion to solve the problem.

$$\frac{\frac{2}{5} \text{ low fat}}{1 \text{ gallon}} = \frac{n \text{ low fat}}{380 \text{ gallons}}$$

While this will give you the correct answer, it is easier to remember that you should multiply to find a fraction of something. It is easier to solve the problem this way.

Fraction (of) × total gallons = low-fat gallons

$$\frac{2}{\underset{1}{\cancel{5}}} \times \frac{\overset{76}{\cancel{380}}}{1} = \frac{2}{1} \times \frac{76}{1} = \textbf{152 gallons}$$

· ·

Underline the necessary information in each problem below. Write the proportions and solve the problems.

1. A slicing machine cut roast beef $\frac{1}{16}$ inch thick. The giant sandwich was advertised to contain roast beef 2 inches thick. How many slices of roast beef were on the sandwich?

2. The La Ronga Bakery baked 1,460 loaves of bread in 1 day. If each loaf contained $1\frac{3}{4}$ teaspoons of salt, how much salt did the bakery use?

3. How many books $\frac{7}{8}$ inch thick can be packed in a box 35 inches deep?

4. A can of pears weighs $9\frac{2}{3}$ ounces. There are 16 cans of pears in a carton. How many ounces does a carton of pears weigh?

5. There are 8 cups of detergent in a bottle of Easy Clean detergent. For one load of laundry, $\frac{1}{4}$ cup is all that is needed. How many loads of laundry can be cleaned with a bottle of Easy Clean?

Solving Conversion Word Problems

Have you ever seen this kind of problem?

EXAMPLE 1 Caren has a 204-**inch** roll of masking tape. How many **feet** of molding can she cover with the roll?

This problem is an example of a type of multiplication or division word problem that contains only one number and requires outside information in order to be solved. These are word problems involving **conversions** from one type of measurement to another.

Here is the solution and explanation of the example.

> **STEP 1** *question:* How many feet?

> **STEP 2** *necessary information:* 204 inches

Notice that the question asks for a solution that has a different label than what is given in the problem. To solve this, you must know how to convert inches to feet. Then you can set up a proportion to solve the problem. You may need to refer to the conversion chart on p. 188.

> **STEP 3** 12 inches = 1 foot
>
> *labels for proportion:* $\dfrac{\text{inches}}{\text{feet}}$
>
> The conversion will be one side of the proportion.
>
> $\dfrac{12 \text{ inches}}{1 \text{ foot}} = \dfrac{204 \text{ inches}}{n \text{ feet}}$

> **STEP 4** Cross multiply.

> **STEP 5** Divide.
>
> $n = \textbf{17 feet}$

$$\frac{12}{1} \times \frac{204}{n}$$

$$12 \times n = 204 \times 1$$
$$12n = 204$$
$$n = \frac{204}{12} = 17$$

A diagram can often help you picture a conversion word problem.

EXAMPLE 2 The Spring Lake Day-Care Center gives each of its 12 children a cup of milk for lunch every day. How many quarts of milk does the center use each day?

STEP 1 *question:* How many quarts of milk does the center use each day?

STEP 2 *necessary information:* 12 cups, 1 cup conversion formula: 4 cups = 1 quart

STEP 3 Decide what arithmetic operation to use.

The diagram shows that you should divide.

number of cups ÷ cups in a quart = number of quarts

STEP 4 Do the arithmetic.

$$12 \text{ cups} \div \frac{4 \text{ cups}}{1 \text{ quart}} = \textbf{3 quarts}$$

STEP 5 Make sure the answer is sensible. Look at the diagram to see that the answer of 3 quarts makes sense.

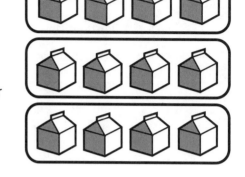

Use the conversion chart on page 188 to help you write the conversion and the proportion for each problem. Then solve the problem.

1. How many years old is Gloria's 30-month-old daughter?

2. A 200-gallon batch of ketchup was bottled in quart bottles. How many bottles were filled?

3. How many kilometers long is a 10,000-meter road race?

4. Paul's truck can carry a $\frac{1}{2}$-ton load. How many pounds of gravel can it carry?

5. José brought the cream shown at the right to the company picnic. How many ounces of cream did he bring?

6. Mt. Everest is 29,028 feet high. How many miles high is Mt. Everest? (Round to the nearest tenth.)

Using Proportions with Fractions and Decimals

Sometimes you will find a multiplication or division word problem in which one number is a decimal and the other is a fraction. The proportion method is very useful in solving this type of word problem.

EXAMPLE   A $\frac{3}{4}$-pound steak cost \$6.75. How much did it cost per pound?

     STEP 1   *question:* How much did it cost per pound?

     STEP 2   *necessary information:* $\frac{3}{4}$ pound, \$6.75

     STEP 3   *labels for proportion:* pound, \$

$$\frac{\frac{3}{4} \text{ pound}}{\$6.75} = \frac{1 \text{ pound}}{\$n}$$

$$\frac{\frac{3}{4}}{6.75} \diagup\!\!\!\!\!\diagdown \frac{1}{n}$$

     STEP 4   Cross multiply.

$$\tfrac{3}{4}n = 6.75$$

     STEP 5   Multiply both sides by $\frac{4}{3}$.

$$n = \overset{2.25}{6.75} \times \frac{4}{3_1}$$

$$n = \mathbf{\$9.00}$$

$$n = 9.00$$

If you had not been able to cancel in the example, you would have multiplied the numerators and divided by the product of the denominators. Keep the decimal point in the correct place.

Write the proportions and solve the problems below. Round money problems to the nearest cent.

1. Cloth was being sold at \$12.60 a yard. Lori bought $3\frac{1}{3}$ yards of cloth. How much did she spend?

2. George was told that 13.5 pounds of time-release fertilizer should last $4\frac{1}{2}$ years. How much fertilizer is used each year?

3. Murray bought $2\frac{2}{3}$ pounds of grapes for \$3.25. How much did the grapes cost per pound?

4. Marty took pictures at graduation. He used $7\frac{1}{2}$ rolls of film and was charged \$384.50. What was the charge per roll of film?

Using Proportions with Multiplication and Division

Underline the necessary information. Write the proportions and solve the problems.

1. A butcher can cut up a chicken in $\frac{1}{12}$ of an hour. How many chickens can be cut up in an 8-hour work day?

2. A nurse can take 8 blood samples in 60 minutes. How long does it take her to take one blood sample?

 3. A mile is about 1.6 kilometers. How many kilometers is a 26-mile marathon?

4. An oil-drilling rig can drill 6 feet in an hour. How far can it drill in 24 hours?

 5. A gram is 0.04 ounces. How many grams are in a 12-ounce can of pineapple juice?

6. Rose uses $3\frac{1}{4}$ pounds of pumpkin to make 2 pumpkin pies. For a fall bake sale, she made 10 pies. How many pounds of pumpkin did she use?

 7. When the floodgates were opened, 68,000 gallons of water flowed over the dam per hour. How many gallons flowed over the dam in a day?

8. Lace trimming costs $0.12 per foot. How much did Zelda spend on $4\frac{1}{4}$ feet of trimming?

9. Super Glue sets in $3\frac{1}{2}$ minutes. In how many seconds does Super Glue set?

10. A 942-page book contained 302,382 words. On the average, how many words were on each page?

STRATEGIES WITH MIXED WORD PROBLEMS

Mixed Word Problems with Whole Numbers

So far, you have worked with word problems that have been divided into two major categories—addition/subtraction problems and multiplication/division problems.

In most situations, you will be faced with the four types of problems mixed together. Always read each problem carefully to get an understanding of the situation it describes. This will help you choose the right arithmetic operation.

Keep these general guidelines in mind:

- when combining amounts   → add

- when finding the difference
  between two amounts   → subtract

- when given one unit of something
  and asked to find several   → multiply

- when asked to find a fraction
  of a quantity   → multiply

- when given the amount for
  several and asked for one   → divide

- when dividing, cutting, sharing   → divide

Working through the following exercises will help sharpen your skills with word problems when the different types are mixed together.

Write the arithmetic operation (addition, subtraction, multiplication, or division) that you would use to solve each problem.
DO NOT SOLVE!

1. Doreen needs 39 credits to complete her bachelor's degree at the state university. The university charges $265 per credit for tuition. How much will Doreen have to pay in tuition if she completes her degree?

2. Alan wrote a 74,200-word manuscript for his new book. The typesetter estimates that there will be an average of 280 words per page. If the typesetter is correct, how many pages will there be in the book?

3. After laying off 27 workers, Paul still had 168 workers at the hospital. How many workers were there at the hospital before the changes?

4. A department store bought shirts for $14 each and sold them for $24. How much profit did it make on each shirt?

5. Tom needs 19 feet of molding for each doorway in his home. The home will have 9 doorways. How much molding does he need?

6. Part of Rob's harvesting log is shown at the right. How many more ears of corn did he harvest on Thursday than on Wednesday?

	WED	THURS
Corn	476	548
Zucchini	94	129

7. As coach of her soccer team, Althea decided that all 22 players would get equal playing time. With a total of 990 minutes to distribute, how many playing minutes did Althea give to each of her players?

8. At her day-care center, Beth used an entire gallon of juice at snack time for 24 children. On the average, how many ounces of juice did each child receive?

9. The governor's goal is to reduce the state's imports of foreign oil by 25,000 barrels to 90,000 barrels a month. How much oil is the state currently importing a month?

Using Labels to Solve Word Problems

Every number in a word problem has a **label.** Every number *refers* to something. In other words, it makes no sense to say simply "7" or "$38\frac{1}{2}$." We need to know—*7 what? $38\frac{1}{2}$ what?* Dogs? Miles per hour? Years old? What do these numbers refer to?

Paying careful attention to labels will help you decide whether to add, subtract, multiply, or divide. Look at the following example.

EXAMPLE 1   On Saturday night, Bruce spent $46.50 on dinner and $38.00 for tickets to a play. How much did he spend altogether?

Notice that the labels of both pieces of the necessary information are *dollars.* Also, you can tell that the label of the answer will be in *dollars.* You probably already have figured out that you need to add $46.50 and $38.00 to solve the problem.

Look at the next example.

EXAMPLE 2   In the last election, 35,102 women and 29,952 men voted. How many people voted?

The labels of the necessary information and the answer are different. Does this mean you should not add or subtract?

Whenever the labels of items in a word problem are different, first ask yourself if the different labels can be part of a *broader category* or if they can be *converted* to a common unit (such as from *pounds* to *ounces* or from *years* to *months*). For example, *men* and *women* can both be considered part of the broader category of *people*; therefore, all the labels in the problem are the same and you can add or subtract to find the answer. For the problem above, you should add 35,102 and 29,952 to get the answer.

Using labels to decide whether to multiply or to divide is a bit trickier. However, if you are willing to play a bit with the labels in a problem, you can often make this decision before you have to work with actual numbers. Read the next example.

> You will often find this pattern in word problems:
>
> When the labels of all the necessary information and the answer are the same, you usually need to *add* or *subtract* to solve.

EXAMPLE 3 Ken drove 385 miles in 7 hours. How many miles per hour did he average on this trip?

The labels of one piece of the necessary information is *miles*; the label of the other piece is *hours*. The label of the answer is *miles per hour*. Already you may be guessing that you should not add or subtract, for the labels are *not* the same and they can't be converted to a common unit.

The answer will be in *miles per hour*, which can also be written as $\frac{miles}{hour}$ (miles *divided by* 1 hour). Set up a statement using the labels from the problem:

$$\text{miles} \,\square\, \text{hours} = \frac{\text{miles}}{\text{hour}}$$

> **Remember:** *miles per hour* means the ratio
> $$\frac{\text{miles}}{\text{hour}}$$

How would you fill in the box? Ask yourself, "What do I have to do to *miles* and *hours* in order to get $\frac{miles}{hour}$?"

You need to divide.

$$385 \text{ miles} \,\boxed{\div}\, 7 \text{ hours} = \frac{\textbf{55 miles}}{\textbf{hour}}$$

OR

$$385 \text{ miles} \div 7 \text{ hours} = \textbf{55 miles per hour}$$

Now look at the next example.

EXAMPLE 4 Ken took a 7-hour trip. He averaged 55 miles per hour on the trip. How many miles in all did he drive?

The label of one piece of the necessary information is *hours*; the label of the other piece is *miles per hour*. The label of the answer will be *miles*. Ask yourself, "What would I do to *hours* and *miles per hour* to get *miles*?"

$$\text{hours} \,\square\, \frac{\text{miles}}{\text{hour}} = \text{miles}$$

Try multiplying. Just as with numerical multiplication, you can cancel out common factors (in this case, the label *hour*).

canceling using words	canceling using numbers
$\cancel{\text{hours}} \,\boxed{\times}\, \dfrac{\text{miles}}{\cancel{\text{hour}}} = \text{miles}$	$\cancel{5} \times \dfrac{3}{\cancel{5}} = 3$

Because canceling labels leaves you the label to your answer, you know that you should multiply to get the correct answer.

$$\cancel{\text{hours}} \;\square\; \frac{\text{miles}}{\cancel{\text{hour}}} = \text{miles}$$

$$7 \;\cancel{\text{hours}} \;\boxed{\times}\; \frac{55 \text{ miles}}{1 \,\cancel{\text{hour}}} = ? \text{ miles}$$

$$7 \times 55 \text{ miles} = \mathbf{385 \text{ miles}}$$

Now, look at a problem in which you can't cancel the labels.

EXAMPLE 5 Ken took a 385-mile trip and drove 55 miles per hour. How many hours did he drive?

Look at the expression. $\text{miles} \;\square\; \dfrac{\text{miles}}{\text{hour}} = \text{hours}$

Can you convert the labels to a common unit? No. Can you cancel the labels *miles* and *hours*? No. You have one more case you should try.

Remember the procedure for dividing fractions is to invert (flip over) the fraction you are dividing by and then multiply the result. You can do the same thing with labels.

$$385 \text{ miles} \;\boxed{\div}\; \frac{55 \text{ miles}}{1 \text{ hour}} = ? \text{ hours}$$

$$385 \;\cancel{\text{miles}} \times \frac{1 \text{ hour}}{55 \,\cancel{\text{miles}}} = ? \text{ hours}$$

$$385 \times \tfrac{1}{55} \text{ hours} = 7 \text{ hours}$$

When you actually do the math, it is easier just to divide, but it is important to know that you can still use the labels to decide which operation to use.

· ·

Read each of the following problems. Look at the labels and decide if they can be renamed to a broader category. Then write in the correct operation to solve the problem. Finally, solve the problem.

1. Sam cut an 8-ounce slice from a 20-pound round of cheese. How many ounces of cheese were left?

    necessary information labels: _____ _____

    answer label: _____

    Are the labels different? _____*yes*_____

    If so, what is the new label? ___*ounces*___

    _____ $\square$ _____ = _____
       label   label   label

    Answer: _____

2. Adrienne needed to cut 2 feet from a 72-inch piece of molding. After the cut, how much molding was left?

   necessary information labels: _____ _____

   answer label: _____

   Are the labels different? _____

   If so, what is the new label? _____

   _____ ☐ _____ = _____
      label   label   label

   Answer: _____

3. Maura's hair was $9\frac{1}{2}$ inches long. How long was her hair before she had cut it by $1\frac{3}{4}$ inches?

   necessary information labels: _____ _____

   answer label: _____

   Are the labels different? _____

   If so, what is the new label? _____

   _____ ☐ _____ = _____
      label   label   label

   Answer: _____

Read the following problems. First look at the labels in the problem and see if they can be canceled. If the labels can't be canceled, flip over the second label, and then check if the labels can be canceled. Then write the correct operation in the box. Finally, solve the problem.

4. A ream of paper contains 500 sheets. A box contains 10 reams of paper. How many sheets of paper are in the box?

   $\dfrac{\text{sheets}}{\text{ream}}$ ☐ reams = sheets   Answer: _____

5. It cost $6 to go to the movies. A movie theater collected $522 in ticket sales. How many tickets were sold?

   dollars ☐ $\dfrac{\text{dollars}}{\text{ticket}}$ = tickets   Answer: _____

6. An average tomato plant in John's garden yields 8 pounds of tomatoes. How much can he expect from his 14 plants?

   plants ☐ $\dfrac{\text{pounds}}{\text{plant}}$ = pounds   Answer: _____

Not Enough Information

Now that you know how to decide whether to add, subtract, multiply, or divide to solve a word problem, you should be able to recognize a word problem that cannot be solved because not enough information is given.

Look at the following example.

EXAMPLE 1 At her waitress job, Sheila earns $4.50 an hour plus tips. Last week she earned $65.40 in tips. How much did she earn last week?

STEP 1 *question:* How much did she earn last week?

STEP 2 *necessary information:* $4.50/hour, $65.40

STEP 3 Decide what arithmetic operation to use.

tips + (pay per hour × hours worked) = total earned

missing information: hours worked

At first glance, you might think that you have enough information since there are two numbers. But when the solution is set up, you can see that you need to know the number of hours Sheila worked to find out what she earned.

For each word problem, circle the letter of the information needed to solve the problem.

1. A supermarket sold 350 pounds of bananas at $0.59 a pound. How many pounds of bananas did it have left?

   a. You need to know how much the supermarket paid for the bananas.
   b. You need to know how many pounds of bananas the supermarket started with.
   c. You need to know how much money the supermarket made for each pound of bananas sold.
   d. You have enough information to solve the problem.

2. In one day last year, 2,417 people were born or moved into the state and 1,620 people died or left the state. What was the state's change of population for the day?

    a. You need to know the total population of the state.
    b. You need to know the name of the state.
    c. You need to know exactly how many people were born and exactly how many died.
    d. You have enough information to solve the problem.

3. Roast beef that normally costs $2.59 a pound was marked down $0.60. If Gina paid for a roast with a $10.00 bill, how much change did she receive?

    a. You need to know the weight of Gina's roast beef.
    b. You need to know the total amount of money Gina had.
    c. You need to know how much the supermarket paid for the roast beef.
    d. You have enough information to solve the problem.

4. A loaded truck carrying boxes of books weighed 7,105 pounds at the weigh station. If each box of books weighed 42 pounds, how much did the unloaded truck weigh?

    a. You need to know how many books were in the truck.
    b. You need to know the weight of a single book.
    c. You need to know how many boxes were in the truck.
    d. You have enough information to solve the problem.

5. A bag of 40 snack bars weighs 12 ounces. How much does each snack bar weigh?

    a. You need to know the price of one snack bar.
    b. You need to know how many ounces are in a pound.
    c. You need to know the total price of the entire bag.
    d. You have enough information to solve the problem.

In the following problems, decide whether to add, subtract, multiply, or divide. Then solve the problem. Circle the letter of the correct answer.

6. Mr. Gomez's obituary appeared in a 1998 newspaper. It said that he was 86 years old when he died and had been married for 51 years. In what year was he born?

   a. 1903
   b. 1947
   c. 1861
   d. 1887
   e. 1912

7. An electrician has a piece of cable the length shown at the right. How long a cable would he have if he laid 7 of these pieces end to end?

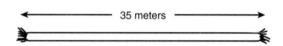

   a. 5 meters
   b. 28 meters
   c. 42 meters
   d. 245 meters
   e. 490 meters

8. The population of San Jose rose by 37,250 people. The population had been 782,250. What was the new population?

   a. 21 times
   b. 745,000 people
   c. 819,500 people
   d. 29,138,812,500 people
   e. not enough information given

9. A Christmas light uses 2 watts of electricity. How many lights can be strung on a circuit that can handle a load of 300 watts?

   a. 150 lights
   b. 600 lights
   c. 298 lights
   d. 302 lights
   e. none of the above

10. A telephone cable can handle 12,500 calls at any one time. How many cables are needed to handle a peak load of 87,500 calls?

    a. 100,000 cables
    b. 75,000 cables
    c. 7 cables
    d. 70 cables
    e. none of the above

11. Gene bought $360 worth of sports equipment and $18 worth of office supplies for the boys' club. Since the boys' club is tax-exempt, he didn't have to pay the sales tax. If he had paid tax, how much would he have spent?

    a. $20
    b. $378
    c. $342
    d. $360
    e. not enough information given

 12. A clothing factory produced 8,760 yards of cloth. What was the average production from each of the 60 looms in the factory?

    a. 146 yards
    b. 1,460 yards
    c. 8,700 yards
    d. 8,820 yards
    e. 525,600 yards

 13. Len's goal was to sell 20 encyclopedias a month. Part of Len's sales log is shown at the right. By how much did he exceed his goal in September?

    a. 57 encyclopedias
    b. 17 encyclopedias
    c. 13 encyclopedias
    d. 2 encyclopedias
    e. 740 encyclopedias

Encyclopedia Sales	
August	19
September	37
October	30
November	21

In the following problems, write a question that matches the solution.

14. In 1996 the per capita income, the average amount of money each person earned, in the District of Columbia was $29,202. Per capita expenses, the average amount of money each person spent, was $26,097.

$29,202 - $26,097 = n$

15. During the pre-Christmas sale, the price of the new car was slashed from $15,364 to $11,994.

$15,364 - $11,994 = n$

16. In order to be stained, concrete needs to be treated with 4 parts muriactic acid mixed with 1 part water. Jaresh had a 1 pint container of muriactic acid.

$$\frac{4 \text{ parts muriactic acid}}{1 \text{ part water}} = \frac{1 \text{ pint muriactic acid}}{n \text{ pints water}}$$

17. When building a roof, Rosalia knew that she needed 1 square foot of ventilation for 300 square feet of attic. Her attic was 1,200 square feet.

$$\frac{1 \text{ sq ft ventilation}}{300 \text{ sq ft attic}} = \frac{n \text{ sq ft ventilation}}{1,200 \text{ sq ft attic}}$$

18. A base coat of stucco uses $2\frac{1}{2}$ parts clean common sand to 1 part Type N cement. Cesar has a 50-pound bucket of Type N cement.

$$\frac{2\frac{1}{2} \text{ parts sand}}{1 \text{ part Type N cement}} = \frac{n \text{ lb sand}}{50 \text{ lb Type N cement}}$$

19. A drill press can drill a hole accurately to 0.002 inch. The press was set to drill a 0.235 hole.

$0.235 \text{ inch} + 0.002 \text{ inch} = n \text{ inch}$

20. Abad and Socorro stayed overnight at Motel 5. The room was $39.95. The motel taxes were $6.25.

$39.95 + $6.25 = n$

Mixed Word Problems—Whole Numbers, Decimals, and Fractions

In the following problems, circle the letter of the correct answer.
Round decimals to the nearest cent or the nearest hundredth.

1. Sandy bought a roast beef sandwich for $1.89, which included
   $0.09 tax. What was the cost of the sandwich alone?

   a. $1.89
   b. $1.80
   c. $1.98
   d. $2.10
   e. $1.70

2. In 1994 the estimated population of the United States was
   260,714,000. The 1994 estimated population of Russia was
   149,609,000. How much greater was the population of the
   United States than the population of Russia?

   a. 111,105,000 people
   b. 410,323,000 people
   c. 129,115,000 people
   d. 309,313,000 people
   e. none of the above

3. To tie her tomato plants, Emmy cut the string shown at the
   right into $\frac{3}{4}$-foot-long pieces. How many pieces of string
   did she have to tie her tomatoes?

   a. $12\frac{3}{4}$ feet
   b. $11\frac{1}{4}$ feet
   c. 9 pieces
   d. 16 pieces
   e. none of the above

4. Boneless chicken breasts cost $1.95 a pound. Cali paid $8.70 for
   a package of chicken breasts. How much did the chicken breasts
   weigh? (Round to nearest hundredth.)

   a. 6.75 pounds
   b. 16.97 pounds
   c. 10.65 pounds
   d. 4.46 pounds
   e. 2.24 pounds

5. At the New York Stock Market, a stock opened at $20\frac{3}{8}$ a share and closed at the end of the day at $22\frac{1}{2}$. How much did it gain for the day?

   a. $42\frac{7}{8}$

   b. $2\frac{1}{8}$

   c. $2\frac{1}{3}$

   d. $2\frac{2}{5}$

   e. none of the above

6. What is the total weight of the two packages of fruit shown at the right?

   a. 1.81 pounds
   b. 1.63 pounds
   c. 2.62 pounds
   d. 1.55 pounds
   e. 0.82 pound

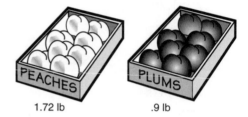

1.72 lb   .9 lb

7. A serving of Kellogg's Raisin Bran contains 0.26 gram of potassium. How many grams of potassium are in an 11-serving package of Raisin Bran?

   a. 11.26 grams
   b. 10.74 grams
   c. 42.31 grams
   d. 2.86 grams
   e. 0.02 gram

8. The auto repair shop charged Muriel $1,125 to repair her car. She had a $250-deductible insurance policy. How much did the insurance company pay for the repair of her car?

   a. $1,375.00
   b. $875.00
   c. $4.50
   d. $281.25
   e. none of the above

9. Debbie spent $\frac{1}{3}$ of her paycheck on food and $\frac{1}{4}$ for clothes. Her paycheck was for $414. How much did she spend for food?

    a. $138.00
    b. $34.50
    c. $241.50
    d. $1,242.00
    e. $103.50

10. State Airlines does a complete maintenance check of its airplanes every 12,000 miles flown. Airplane #200 was flown 96,000 miles last year. How many complete maintenance checks did it have last year?

    a. 480 maintenance checks
    b. 84,000 miles
    c. 108,000 miles
    d. 8 maintenance checks
    e. 1,152,000,000 miles

11. After getting a tune-up, Ernie was able to drive 283.1 miles on 14.9 gallons of gas. How many miles did he get per gallon?

    a. 19 miles
    b. 42.18 miles
    c. 134 miles
    d. 298 miles
    e. 268.2 miles

12. The Platte River is normally 7 feet deep. During a recent flood, it crested at 14 feet above normal. What was the depth of the river at the crest of the flood?

    a. 7 feet
    b. 21 feet
    c. 98 feet
    d. 2 feet
    e. none of the above

13. The *Concorde* flew 3,855 miles across the Atlantic in $3\frac{3}{4}$ hours. What was its average speed?

    a. $3,858\frac{3}{4}$ miles per hour
    b. $3,851\frac{1}{4}$ miles per hour
    c. 1,028 miles per hour
    d. $14,456\frac{1}{3}$ miles per hour
    e. $467\frac{9}{33}$ miles per hour

PERCENT WORD PROBLEMS

Identifying the Parts of a Percent Word Problem

Read the statements below.

The 8-ounce glass is 50% full. It contains 4 ounces.

These statements contain three facts:

the whole: the 8-ounce glass

the part: 4 ounces

the percent: 50%

A one-step percent word problem would be missing one of these facts. When you are solving a percent word problem, first identify what you are looking for. As shown above, you have three possible choices: *the part, the whole,* or *the percent.*

It is usually easiest to figure out that you are being asked to find the percent. Word problems asking for the percent usually ask for it directly, with a question such as "What is the percent?" or "Find the percent" or "Three is what percent?" Occasionally, other percent-type words are used, such as "What is the *interest rate*?"

EXAMPLE 1   What percent of 30 is 6?

The question asks *is what percent?* Therefore, you are looking for the percent.

Sometimes you are given the percent and one other number. You must decide whether you are looking for the part or the whole.

EXAMPLE 2   81% of what number is 162?

The phrase *of what number* means you are looking for the whole.

EXAMPLE 3 Yesterday 114 city employees were absent. This was 4% of the city work force. How many people work for the city?

    STEP 1 *question:* How many people work for the city?

    STEP 2 *necessary information:* 114 city employees, 4%

    STEP 3 You are given the number of city employees who were absent (114) and the percent of the work force that this represents (4%). You are looking for the total number of people who work for the city, the whole.

EXAMPLE 4 What number is 75% of 40?

You are looking for a number that is a percent of another number. You are looking for the part.

EXAMPLE 5 Operating at full capacity, the automobile plant produced 25 cars an hour. How many cars did the plant produce when operating at 40% capacity?

    STEP 1 *question:* How many cars did the plant produce?

    STEP 2 *necessary information:* 25 cars, 40%

    STEP 3 You are given the production at full capacity (25 cars an hour). To find the production at 40% capacity, you solve for the part.

For each problem, write down whether you are looking for the part, the whole, or the percent. DO NOT SOLVE!

1. The city reported that 14,078 out of 35,817 registered voters voted in the election. What percent of registered voters voted in the election?

2. A total of 14,615 people voted in the election. The election results are shown at the right. How many votes did the winning candidate get?

Vote Percentages	
Candidate A	54%
Candidate B	39%
Candidate C	7%

3. An ad said that 36% of the plumbers polled recommended Drāno. If 72 plumbers recommended Drāno, how many plumbers were polled?

4. Eric found that 85% of a roll of 36 pictures were perfect prints. How many perfect prints did he get from the roll?

5. A seed company guaranteed 87% germination of its spinach seed. If Jed had 450 spinach seeds germinate, how many seeds did he plant?

6. The state had a work force of 1,622,145. If 132,998 of these people were unemployed, what was the unemployment rate for the state?

7. A bedroom set normally priced at $1,400 is on sale. How much would Rochelle save if she bought the set at the advertised sale, shown at the right, instead of at the regular price?

8. Last year, 980 people took the high school equivalency exam at the local official test center. If 637 people passed the exam, what percent of the people taking the exam passed?

9. If 8% of the registered voters sign the initiative petition, it will be placed on the November ballot. There are 193,825 registered voters in the county. How many of them must sign the petition for it to go on the ballot?

10. An independent study group estimated that only 35% of all crimes in the city were reported. Last year 2,800 crimes were reported. According to the study, how many crimes were actually committed?

Solving Percent Word Problems

Once you identify what you are looking for in a percent word problem, set up the problem and solve it.

Percent word problems can be solved using proportions. These problems can be set up in the following form:

$$\frac{\text{part}}{\text{whole}} = \frac{\%}{100}$$

This proportion means that the ratio of the part to the whole is equal to the ratio of the percent to 100.

Using the proportion method, you can solve for the part, the whole, or the percent. The percent is always written over 100 because the percent represents a fraction with 100 in the denominator.

As you saw in your earlier work with proportions, a proportion is the same as two equivalent fractions. For example,

2 is 50% of 4 and can be written as

$$\frac{2}{4} = \frac{50\%}{100}$$

2 is the *part*, 4 is the *whole*, and 50 is the *percent*.

EXAMPLE 1 4 is what percent of 16?

STEP 1 *question:* is what percent?

You are looking for the percent.

STEP 2 *necessary information:* 4 is, of 16

For this type of percent exercise, the word *is* follows the part, and the number after *of* is the whole.

STEP 3 Set up a proportion in this form:

numbers   *percents*

$$\frac{\text{part}}{\text{whole}} = \frac{\text{percent}}{100}$$

Fill in the proportion with the given information from the problem. Call the number you are looking for *n*.

numbers   *percents*

$$\frac{4}{16} = \frac{n}{100}$$

STEP 4   Cross multiply.

$$16 \times n = 4 \times 100$$
$$16n = 400$$

STEP 5   Divide.

$$n = \frac{400}{16} = 25\%$$

EXAMPLE 2   If 24 out of 96 city playgrounds need major repairs, what percent of the city playgrounds need major repairs?

STEP 1   *question:* What percent of the city playgrounds need major repairs?

You are looking for the percent.

STEP 2   *necessary information:* 24 out of 96

96 is the whole (all the playgrounds).

24 is the part (playgrounds needing repairs).

STEP 3   *numbers*   *percents*

$$\frac{24 \text{ playgrounds}}{96 \text{ playgrounds}} = \frac{n}{100}$$

STEP 4   Cross multiply.

$$96 \times n = 24 \times 100$$
$$96n = 2,400$$

STEP 5   Divide.

$$n = \frac{2,400}{96} = 25\%$$

EXAMPLE 3   30% of what number is 78?

STEP 1   *question:* of what number?

You are looking for the whole.

STEP 2   *necessary information:* 30%, is 78

30% is the percent.

78 is the part.

STEP 3   Set up a proportion.

$$\frac{78}{n} = \frac{30}{100}$$

STEP 4   Cross multiply.

$$30 \times n = 78 \times 100$$
$$30n = 7,800$$

STEP 5   Divide.

$$n = \frac{7,800}{30} = 260$$

EXAMPLE 4 The finance company required that Lynn make a down payment of 15% on a used car. She can afford a down payment of $600. What is the most expensive car that she could buy?

STEP 1 *question:* What is the most expensive car that she could buy?

You are looking for the whole (the price of the car).

STEP 2 *necessary information:* 15%, $600

15% is the percent.
$600 is the down payment, which is a part of the total price of the car.

STEP 3 Set up a proportion.

$$\frac{\$600}{\$n} = \frac{15}{100}$$

STEP 4 Cross multiply.

$$15 \times n = 600 \times 100$$
$$15n = 60{,}000$$

STEP 5 Divide.

$$n = \frac{60{,}000}{15} = \$4{,}000$$

EXAMPLE 5 What is 40% of 65?

STEP 1 *question:* What is?

You are looking for the part.

STEP 2 *necessary information:* 40%, of 65

40% is the percent.

65 is the whole.

STEP 3 Set up a proportion.

$$\frac{n}{65} = \frac{40}{100}$$

STEP 4 Cross multiply.

$$100 \times n = 65 \times 40$$
$$100n = 2{,}600$$

STEP 5 Divide.

$$n = \frac{2{,}600}{100} = 26$$

EXAMPLE 6 June decided that she could spend 25% of her income for rent. She makes $1,740 a month. How much can she spend for rent?

STEP 1 *question:* How much can she spend for rent?

You are looking for the part of her income that she will spend on rent.

STEP 2 *necessary information:* 25%, $1,740

25% is the percent.
$1,740 is her whole income.

STEP 3 Set up a proportion.

$$\frac{\$n}{\$1,740} = \frac{25}{100}$$

STEP 4 Cross multiply.

$$100 \times n = 1,740 \times 25$$
$$100n = 43,500$$

STEP 5 Divide.

$$n = \frac{43,500}{100} = \$435$$

Use proportions to solve the following problems.

1. 36 is what percent of 144?

2. 288 is 72% of what number?

3. What is 68% of 75?

4. A $160 suit was reduced by $40. What was the percent of the reduction?

5. The election results are shown at right. If 28,450 votes were cast in the school board election, how many votes did Marsha receive?

6. The state government cut aid for adult education by 25%. Metropolis expects to lose $96,000. How much aid for adult education had Metropolis been receiving?

7. Last year Jeffrey paid 7% of his income in taxes. He paid $1,659. What was his income?

School Board Elections

Clayton	19%
Andrea	21%
Marcus	2%
Marsha	58%

8. Exactly 60% of the residents of the city are African American. The population of the city is 345,780. How many African American people live in the city?

9. In 1998, Robyn paid $340 interest on $2,000 that she had borrowed. What was the interest rate on the borrowed money?

10. In order to control his chloresterol, Sespend tried to limit his calories from fat to 20% of his total calories. On an average day, he eats 2,400 calories. What is the most calories from fat he can eat on an average day if he is to meet his goal?

For each word problem, select the correct question that matches the solution.

11. Khan had a special coupon that allowed her to take 20% off the price of a clearance item. She decided to buy a sweater she wanted that had a clearance price of $16.

    a. How much did she pay for the sweater?
    b. How much money did she have left?
    c. How much did she save with her coupon?
    d. What was the original price of the sweater?
    e. How many sweaters could she buy?

    $$\frac{\$n}{\$16} = \frac{20\%}{100}$$
    $$n = \frac{320}{100} = \$3.20$$

12. A national survey found that 720 out of 900 dentists recommended using Never Breaks dental floss.

    a. How many dentists recommended a different brand?
    b. How many more dentists recommended Never Break than all other brands?
    c. How many different brands were recommended?
    d. What percent of dentists recommended other brands?
    e. What percent of dentists recommended Never Break?

    $$\frac{720 \text{ dentists}}{900 \text{ dentists}} = \frac{n\%}{100}$$
    $$900n = 72,000$$
    $$n = \frac{72,000}{900} = 80\%$$

13. The state passed a law requiring 60% of legislators to vote for a tax increase in order for it to pass. The lower house had 180 members.

   a. At least how many legislators in the lower house had to support a tax increase in order for it to pass?
   b. At least how many legislators in the lower house had to oppose a tax increase in order for it not to pass?
   c. What was the largest number of legislators that could oppose a tax increase that passes in the lower house?
   d. How many more legislators are needed to pass a tax increase in the lower house than when only a 50% majority was needed?
   e. What was the smallest possible margin of victory?

   $$\frac{n \text{ members}}{180 \text{ members}} = \frac{60\%}{100}$$

   $$100n = 10{,}800$$

   $$n = 108 \text{ legislators}$$

14. Floor Mart advertised a total savings of 30% off list price for their store brand microwave oven. When Wilson bought the microwave oven, he saved $75 from the list price.

   a. What percent of the list price did he pay?
   b. What was the list price of the oven?
   c. What was the sale price of the oven?
   d. How much change did Wilson receive?
   e. How much more would he have paid if he had paid full price?

   $$\frac{\$75}{\$n} = \frac{30\%}{100}$$

   $$30n = 7500$$

   $$n = \frac{7500}{30} = \$250$$

15. The production line for the molded plastic parts needs to be stopped and the machines readjusted if 2% or more of the parts are rejected by the inspectors. In an hour, 600 parts are made on the production line.

   a. What is the largest number of parts that can be defective in an hour?
   b. What is the smallest number of parts that can be defective in an hour?
   c. What is the largest possible number of good parts that can be made in an hour in which the production line needs to be stopped?
   d. What is the smallest possible number of defective parts that need to be found in an hour in order to shut down the production line?
   e. How many more good parts than rejected parts were produced?

   $$\frac{n \text{ parts}}{600 \text{ parts}} = \frac{2\%}{100}$$

   $$100n = 1200$$

   $$n = 12 \text{ parts}$$

Percent and Estimation

Have you ever listened to a report of election results? The reporter will often say something like, "The Congressman was reelected with 54% of the vote." This percent is an estimate, not an exact amount. The reporter has rounded the result to the nearest percent.

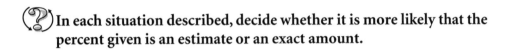 **In each situation described, decide whether it is more likely that the percent given is an estimate or an exact amount.**

1. The state unemployment rate was 5.3% last month.

   a. exact
   b. estimate

2. During the sale, all clothing prices are reduced 20%.

   a. exact
   b. estimate

3. Scientists say that there is a 15% chance of a major earthquake in the region in the next ten years.

   a. exact
   b. estimate

4. Even 20 years after the last underground nuclear tests, background radiation levels were 35% above normal.

   a. exact
   b. estimate

5. Angel's son Alberto got a grade of 88% correct on the 50-question multiple-choice test.

   a. exact
   b. estimate

6. In the city, 24% of the people were living in poverty.

   a. exact
   b. estimate

For each word problem, find a solution that could be true. Some questions have a range of possible correct answers. Others have only one possible correct answer.

7. The newscast reported that Elena received 65% of the vote in the local election in which 4,864 votes were cast. How many votes might she have received?

8. The official report said that the city population was expected to increase 5% in the next decade. The current population is 128,431. What could the population be in a decade and still be within the predicted range?

9. The investment analyst predicted a 12% return on the mutual fund. Sugi invested $3,000 and at the end of the year had earned $352 on that investment. Was the prediction accurate?

10. The state printed 20,000,000 Instant Winner Lottery Tickets and claimed that 3% of the tickets were winners, with the prizes ranging from a free ticket to $100,000. How many winning tickets were printed?

11. An Internet provider predicted that its number of customers would increase 18% in a year. At the start of the year, the company had 56,820 customers. At the end of the year, it had 69,965 customers. Was the Internet provider's prediction accurate?

The Percent Circle

If you find working with proportions to solve percent problems too abstract, you could use a memory aid called the **percent circle.** The percent circle is equivalent to a proportion, but it creates a picture to help you decide whether to multiply or divide.

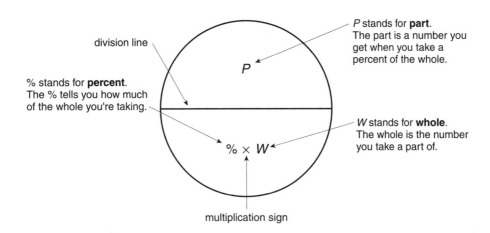

division line

P stands for **part.**
The part is a number you get when you take a percent of the whole.

% stands for **percent.**
The % tells you how much of the whole you're taking.

W stands for **whole.**
The whole is the number you take a part of.

multiplication sign

Using the Percent Circle

<u>EXAMPLE 1</u> Finding a part of the whole.

According to Francisco's union contract, he is due to get a 4% raise. He currently earns $350 a week. What will his raise be?

STEP 1 The raise is calculated as a part of his salary. Therefore cover *P* (the part) since that is the number you're trying to find.

STEP 2 Read the uncovered symbols: $\% \times W$.

To find the part, multiply the percent by the whole.

STEP 3 Write the percent as either a fraction or a decimal.

$$4\% = \frac{4}{10} \text{ or } 0.04$$

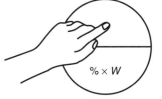

STEP 4 Do the calculation.

$$\frac{4}{100} \times 350 = \frac{1400}{100} = \$14 \text{ or } 0.04 \times 350 = \$14.00$$

Francisco will get a **$14 raise.**

> **Note:** When you use the percent circle, you must remember that *percent* means "compared to 100." When you know the percent, remember to divide it by 100. When you are looking for the percent, remember to multiply by 100.

__EXAMPLE 2__ Finding a whole when a part and a percent are given.

The Cheap Cars used car lot requires buyers to pay 20% of the total price of a car as a down payment. The buyer can finance the rest of the purchase price. Celso can spend up to $800 on a down payment for a used car. What is the highest price used car he could buy at Cheap Cars?

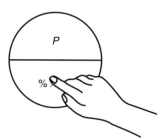

STEP 1   Since the down payment is a part of the price of a car, you are trying to find the whole. Therefore, cover W (the whole) since that is the number you're trying to find.

STEP 2   Read the uncovered symbols. $\frac{P}{\%}$ means $P \div \%$.

To find the whole, divide the part by the percent.

STEP 3   Write the percent as either a fraction or a decimal.

$$20\% = \frac{20}{100} = \frac{1}{5} \text{ or } 0.20$$

STEP 4   Do the calculation.

$$800 \div \frac{1}{5} = 800 \times \frac{5}{1} = \$4,000, \text{ or } 20\overline{)800.00}^{\,\$4000}$$

The highest price used car Celso could buy at Cheap Cars would cost **$4,000.**

__EXAMPLE 3__ Finding what percent a part is of a whole.

A clinic tested 360 drug abusers for HIV and found that 284 tested positive. What percent of the drug abusers tested HIV positive?

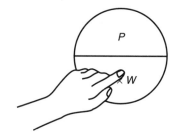

STEP 1   You need to find what percent 234 is of 360.
You are looking for the percent. Therefore cover %.

STEP 2   Read the uncovered symbols. $\frac{P}{W}$ means $P \div W$.

To find the percent, divide the part by the whole.

STEP 3   Do the calculation.

$$\frac{234}{360} \text{ or } 360\overline{)234.00}^{\,0.65}$$

STEP 4   Convert the decimal to a percent.

$$0.65 \times 100 = 65\%$$

65% of the drug abusers tested HIV positive.

Note: It is possible for the part to be larger than the whole. If the part is larger than the whole, the percent will be larger than 100%.

Use the percent circle to solve the following word problems.

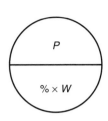

1. Dinner cost Luis $40. He wanted to leave the waitress a 15% tip. How much should he leave for a tip?

2. Armand bought a chain saw for $80. How much did he pay in sales tax if the sales tax was 5%?

3. Webmasters Computer Company has 540 employees. Of those employees, 27 are over age 60. What percent of the employees are over age 60?

4. Super Foods' market research showed that 2% of all households that received a weekly circular actually came to shop at the store. The store manager of a new Super Foods planned for 1,500 different customers to visit the Super Foods store in its first week. How many circulars should she plan to send out?

5. Ninety days after the end of training, 24 out of 30 graduates of the computer repair training program had found jobs. What was the job placement rate of the computer repair training program?

6. The Serious Disease Charity spent $28,000 to raise $112,000 in contributions. What percent of the money raised was spent on fund raising?

Solving Percent Word Problems with Decimals and Fractions

Many percent word problems also contain decimals or fractions.
These problems are also solved using the proportion method.

EXAMPLE 1   What is $33\frac{1}{3}$% of 54?

STEP 1   *question:* What is?

You are looking for the part.

STEP 2   *necessary information:* $33\frac{1}{3}$%, of 54

$33\frac{1}{3}$ is the percent.

54 is the whole.

STEP 3   *proportion:*

$$\frac{n}{54} = \frac{33\frac{1}{3}}{100}$$

STEP 4   Cross multiply and divide.

$$100 \times n = 33\frac{1}{3} \times 54$$
$$100n = 1{,}800$$
$$n = \frac{1{,}800}{100} = 18$$

EXAMPLE 2   Bob takes home $156.40 out of his weekly pay of $184.00.
What percent of his pay does he take home?

STEP 1   *question:* What percent of his pay does he take home?

You are looking for the percent.

STEP 2   *necessary information:* $156.40, $184.00

$156.40 is the part.
$184.00 is the whole.

STEP 3   *proportion:*

$$\frac{\$156.40}{\$184.00} = \frac{n}{100}$$

STEP 4   Cross multiply and divide.

$$184 \times n = 156.40 \times 100$$
$$184n = 15{,}640$$
$$n = \frac{15{,}640}{184} = 85\%$$

You can also use the percent circle to solve percent word problems with fractions or decimals.

EXAMPLE 3 Specialty Hardware needs to collect 6% sales tax on all items. In one day the store collected $424.80 in taxes. What were the store's total sales for the day?

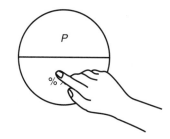

STEP 1 Since you are looking for the total sales for the day and you know the taxes collected and the tax rate, you are looking for the whole. Therefore, cover W (the whole) since that is the number you're trying to find.

STEP 2 Use the percent circle. $\frac{P}{\%}$ means $P \div \%$.

To find the whole, divide the part by the percent.

STEP 3 Convert the percent to a fraction or a decimal.

$6\% = \frac{6}{100}$ or 0.06

STEP 4 Do the calculation.

$$424.80 \div \frac{6}{100} = 424.80 \times \frac{100}{6} = \frac{42480}{6} = \$7,080, \text{ or } .06\overline{)424.80}^{\;\$7,080}$$

The total sales for the day were **$7,080.**

· ·

 Solve the following percent problems using proportions or the percent circle.

1. 4.5% of what number is 90?

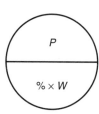

2. $\frac{1}{10}$ is what percent of $\frac{3}{4}$?

3. $66\frac{2}{3}\%$ of what number is 42?

4. What is 6.4% of 800?

5. Russo's Restaurant collected $49.76 in taxes Friday night. The food tax is 8%. How much money did the restaurant receive for meals on Friday night?

For problems 6–8, use the tax guidelines chart shown at the right.

> **State Tax Guidelines**
>
> Clothing—6%
> Food—5%
> Alcohol—7%
> Cigarettes—8%

6. Jed bought a steak dinner for $8.60. Find the amount of tax he paid.

7. Sylvia bought a skirt for $42.50. Find the amount of tax she paid.

8. Flavia bought a bottle of wine costing $15.95 for a dinner party. Find the amount of tax she paid.

9. Glenda bought maple syrup for $1.92 a pint and sold the syrup for $0.96 a pint more. By what percent did she mark up the price of the maple syrup?

10. Barnes and Noble was having a storewide book sale in which all prices were cut $12\frac{1}{2}$%. How much did Juan save on a book that normally costs $12.80?

11. A telemarketing company found that 3.5% of its calls resulted in new subscribers. If its target is 12,000 new subscribers, how many calls should the company plan to make?

Solving Percent Word Problems

The following problems give you a chance to review percent word problems containing whole numbers, decimals, and fractions.

Solve the problems by using proportions or the percent circle.

1. Of the dentists surveyed, 3 out of 4 recommend a fluoride toothpaste. What percent of the dentists surveyed recommend a fluoride toothpaste?

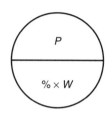

2. Of the registered voters, 112,492 people voted for mayor in the city. This was 40% of the registered voters. How many registered voters are there in the city?

3. In a normal season, the Seaside Resort has 34,500 visitors. This year, due to bad weather, 11,500 fewer visitors came to the resort. What was the percent drop in business for the resort?

4. The High Tech Electronics Company announced an 8.6% profit on sales of $49,600,000. How much profit did the company make?

5. The Quality Chocolate Company decided to increase the size of its chocolate bar 0.4 ounce. This was an increase in size of $16\frac{2}{3}\%$. What was the weight of its chocolate bar before the change?

6. In a recent flu epidemic, 0.8% of people over age 65 who caught the disease died. The death toll in this group was 40. How many people over age 65 caught the flu?

7. In 2000, Dennis paid 13% of his income in taxes. How much did he pay in income taxes that year according to the chart at the right?

Yearly Earnings Dennis Ferguson	
1999	$10,048
2000	$11,694
2001	$12,509

8. The Machinist's Union has just won a 7% raise for its members. Dan is a union member who was making $17,548. How much of a raise will he get?

9. Nayana received a 9% raise worth $18 a week. What had her week's salary been?

10. Basketball star Kareem scored on 506 out of 1,012 attempts. What was his scoring percentage?

11. A $\frac{3}{4}$-cup serving of Honey Nut Cheerios served with skim milk provides 30% of the U.S. recommended daily allowance of vitamin A. How many cups of Honey Nut Cheerios should you eat in order to receive the full U.S. recommended daily allowance of vitamin A when you have skim milk with each serving?

12. A $3\frac{3}{4}$-ounce serving of Norway Sardines in chili sauce provides 100% of the U.S. recommended daily allowance for vitamin D. What percent of the U.S. daily allowance is provided per ounce of the Norway Sardines in chili sauce?

COMBINATION WORD PROBLEMS

Solving Combination Word Problems

Until now, this book has shown you one-step word problems. However, many situations require you to use a combination of math operations to solve word problems.

Generally, you can solve these combination problems by breaking them into two or more one-step problems. As you read a word problem, you may see that it will take more than one math operation to solve. The difficulty lies in deciding how many steps to take and in what order to work them out.

The key to solving combination problems is—

start with the question and work backward.

This shouldn't be difficult. Throughout this book, you have started your work with finding the question.

Follow these steps in solving combination word problems.

STEP 1 Find the question.

STEP 2 Select the necessary information.

STEP 3 Write a solution sentence for the problem. Fill in only the necessary information that belongs in the solution sentence.

Write another sentence, this time to find the information that is missing in the solution sentence. Solve the sentence that gives you the missing information.

STEP 4 Fill in the missing information (the answer from Step 3) in the solution sentence and solve.

STEP 5 Make sure that the answer is sensible.

No matter how many short problems a combination problem consists of, you can always work backward from the solution sentence. Examples 1 and 2 illustrate this.

EXAMPLE 1   Sengchen had $38 in her checking account. She wrote checks for $14 and $9. How much money was left in her checking account?

STEP 1   *question:* How much money was left in her checking account?

STEP 2   *necessary information:* $38, $14, $9

STEP 3   Write a solution sentence.

money − checks = money left

Fill in the sentence with information that can be used to solve the problem.

$$\$38 - checks = money\ left$$

Decide what *missing information* is needed to solve the problem. Write a number sentence and solve.

check + check = checks

$14 + $9 = $\boxed{\$23}$

Now you have the complete information needed to solve the problem.

$$\$38 - \boxed{\$23} = money\ left$$

STEP 4   Solve.

$$\$38 - \$23 = \$15\ left$$

EXAMPLE 2   Lillie worked as a travel agent. She arranged a trip for 56 people at a cost of $165 for airfare plus $230 for hotel per person. How much money did she collect from the group?

STEP 1   *question:* How much money did she collect?

STEP 2   *necessary information:* 56 people, $165 airfare, $230 hotel accommodations

STEP 3   Write a solution sentence.

cost × number of people = total

$$cost \times 56 = total$$

Solve for *missing information.*

airfare + hotel = cost

$165 + $230 = $\boxed{\$395}$

$$\boxed{\$395} \times 56 = total\ cost$$

STEP 4   Solve.

$$\$395 \times 56 = \$22{,}120\ total$$

The words that you use in the solution and missing information sentences may differ from what is presented here. What is important is that you break down the problem into smaller steps.

A combination word problem that needs both multiplication and division to be solved can often be written as one proportion instead of two separate word sentences.

EXAMPLE 3   Apples were sold at a cost of 58 cents for 2 pounds. How much did Michelle pay for 3 pounds of apples?

STEP 1   *question:* How much did Michelle pay for 3 pounds of apples?

STEP 2   *necessary information:* 2 pounds, 58 cents, 3 pounds

STEP 3   Write a proportion to show the relationship between weight and cost.

STEP 4   Fill in the appropriate numbers and solve.

$$\frac{pounds}{cents} = \frac{pounds}{cents}$$

$$\frac{2\ pounds}{58\ cents} = \frac{3\ pounds}{n}$$

$$2 \times n = 3 \times 58$$

$$n = \frac{174}{2} = 87\ cents$$

After some practice, you will be able to tell which problems can be solved with a proportion. In most cases, breaking down a problem into smaller problems with word sentences will be the best method for solution.

....

For each word problem, write two word sentences (a solution sentence and a missing information sentence) or a proportion. DO NOT SOLVE!

1. Tim earns $380 a week. Every week $149 in taxes and $16 in union dues are taken out of his paycheck. What is his take-home pay?

2. After starting the day with $41, Miguel spent $3 for lunch and $22 for gas. How much money did he have left by the end of the day?

3. A store bought 30 boxes of dolls for $720. If there were 8 dolls in a box, how much did each doll cost?

4. Samuel had $394 in his checking account. After he wrote a check for $187 and deposited $201, how much money was in his checking account?

5. Kelly bought five of the blouses shown at the right and one skirt. How much money did she spend on these clothes?

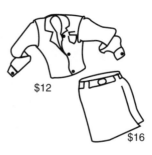

$12

$16

6. Martha borrowed $4,600 to buy a new car. She will have to pay $728 interest. She plans to pay back the loan plus the interest in 24 equal monthly payments. How much will her monthly payments be?

7. To be hired, a data entry operator must be able to enter numbers into a computer at the rate of 10,000 numbers every 60 minutes. Yvana took a 15-minute data entry test. How many numbers did she have to enter to be hired?

8. A 14-gram serving of Cain's Mayonnaise contains 5 grams of polyunsaturated fat and 2 grams of saturated fat. How many grams of saturated fat are there in a 224-gram jar of Cain's Mayonnaise?

9. At Burger Queen, a cheeseburger costs $1.89, medium french fries cost $1.29, and a medium cola costs $1.19. The cheeseburger combination meal of a cheeseburger, medium fries, and medium cola costs $4.29. How much does Olga save by buying the cheeseburger combination meal instead of buying the three items separately?

Write two one-step word sentences or a proportion needed to solve the following combination word problems. Then solve the problems.

10. For the convention, each of the 8 wards of the city elected 4 delegates, while 5 delegates were elected at large. How many delegates did the city send to the convention?

11. It cost the gas station owner $81 in parts and $45 in labor to fix his customer's car. He charged his customer $163. How much profit did the owner make on the job?

12. Mark was offered a job downtown that would give him a raise of $78 a month over his current salary, but his commuting costs would be $2 a day higher. If he works 22 days a month, what would be his net monthly increase in pay?

13. The recipe at the right serves 6 people. Ginny is planning to make the recipe for 8 people. How much stew beef does she need?

> ### Hearty Stew
>
> 3 cups beef stock
> 1 cup red wine
> $\frac{1}{4}$ cup oil
> 2 pounds potatoes
> 3 pounds stew beef
> 1 pound carrots

14. Last month Elvira was billed $60 for using 720 kilowatts of electricity. This month she checked her meter and found that she had used 648 kilowatts of electricity. Assuming the cost of electricity has not changed, what will her electric bill be for this month?

15. Carlos has a large landscaping job that requires 1,728 cubic feet of loam. His pickup truck can carry 48 cubic feet of loam. He can deliver 6 loads of loam each workday. How many workdays will it take Carlos to deliver all the loam he needs for his landscaping job?

Solving Problems with Decimals, Fractions, Percents

Decimal, fraction, and percent combination word problems are set up and solved in the same way as whole-number combination word problems.

EXAMPLE 1 For each child at her daughter's birthday party, Shelly spent $0.35 for a party favor and $0.16 for a balloon. She had 13 children at the party. How much did she spend for gifts for the children?

> **STEP 1** *question:* How much did she spend for gifts for the children?
>
> **STEP 2** *necessary information:* $0.35, $0.16, 13 children
>
> **STEP 3** *solution sentences:*
>
> gifts × children = total cost
>
> *missing information sentence:*
>
> favor + balloon = gifts
>
> $0.35 + $0.16 = $0.51
>
> **STEP 4** Solve.

$$gifts \times 13 = total\ cost$$

$$\$0.51 \times 13 = total\ cost$$
$$\$0.51 \times 13 = \$6.63$$

EXAMPLE 2 Bright's department store advertised that everything in the store was $\frac{1}{5}$ off. Debbie bought a pair of pants labeled $20. How much did the pants cost her?

> **STEP 1** *question:* How much did the pants cost her?
>
> **STEP 2** *necessary information:* $\frac{1}{5}$, $20
>
> **STEP 3** *solution sentence:*
>
> original price – discount = sale price
>
> *missing information sentence:*
>
> price × fraction = discount
>
> $20 × $\frac{1}{5}$ = $4 discount
>
> **STEP 4** Solve.

$$\$20 - discount = sale\ price$$

$$\$20 - \$4 = sale\ price$$
$$\$20 - \$4 = \$16$$

Both of these examples illustrate two-step word problems. Later in this chapter you will work with problems that need more than two steps for solution.

EXAMPLE 3 Real Value Hardware advertised that all prices had been reduced 15%. A socket set is on sale for $13.60. What was its original price?

STEP 1 *question:* What was its original price?

STEP 2 *necessary information:* 15%, $13.60

STEP 3 *solution statement:* Since this is a percent problem, you can write a proportion.

$$\frac{\text{part}}{\text{whole}} = \frac{\text{percent}}{100}$$

$$\frac{13.60}{n} = \frac{percent}{100}$$

missing information:

100% – percent reduced = percent sale

100% – 15% = 85%

$$\frac{13.60}{n} = \frac{85}{100}$$

$$85 \times n = 13.60 \times 100$$

STEP 4 Solve.

$$85n = 1{,}360$$

$$n = \$16$$

Write two one-step word sentences or a proportion needed to solve the following combination word problems. Then solve the problems.

1. Chris bought 6 boxes of cookies for $14.40. If there were 20 cookies in a box, how much did each cookie cost?

2. The $400 washing machine at the right was reduced for clearance. What was its sale price?

3. Beverly bought five cans of pears, each containing $9\frac{3}{4}$ ounces of pears, and one can of fruit cocktail containing $17\frac{1}{2}$ ounces of fruit. What was the total weight of the fruit she bought?

4. A water widget cost Phil $2.49. Because it reduced his use of hot water, it saved him $3.40 a month in costs for hot water. What were his net savings for 12 months?

5. When cooked, a hamburger loses $\frac{1}{3}$ of its original weight. How much does a $\frac{1}{4}$-pound hamburger weigh after it is cooked?

6. The tax on a meal is 6%. How much is Milton's total bill on a $24 dinner?

7. During the summer clearance sale, everything in the store was 30% off. Solaire bought the bathing suit advertised at the right. How much did she pay for the suit?

> ### 30% Off the Prices Below!
>
> Shorts—regularly $10.50
> Shirts—regularly $9.00
> Socks—regularly $1.99
> Bathing Suits—regularly $19.50

8. Marlene bought a new couch for $310.60. She paid $130 down and planned to pay the rest in 12 equal monthly payments. How much will she pay each month?

9. Walter bought a case of 30 bottles of cooking oil for $57.00. He then sold the oil for $2.10 per bottle. How much money did he make on each bottle?

10. Walter bought a case of 30 bottles of cooking oil for $57.00. He then sold the oil for a profit of $0.20 per bottle. What was the percent of profit? (Round to the nearest tenth of a percent.)

11. At her diner, Mireya added 0.2 ounce of salt to her 4 gallon (256 ounce) pot of beef stew. How much salt was in each 12-ounce portion?

12. A clothing manufacturer makes a blouse and matching skirt. The manufacturer buys material for the clothes in 60-inch-wide rolls. Each skirt pattern requires $\frac{2}{3}$ yard of material, while each blouse requires $1\frac{1}{4}$ yards of material. How many complete outfits can be made from a 70-yard-long roll of material?

Order of Operations

You've seen how to use solution sentences to solve combination word problems. If you know and use the rules for order of operations, you can write out the steps of a multistep word problem in one line.

Following are the rules for order of operations in arithmetic expressions.

Rule 1: Do multiplication and division before addition and subtraction.

EXAMPLE 1 $9 - 2 \times 4$

> **SOLUTION:** Multiply. $2 \times 4 = 8$
>
> Subtract. $9 - 8 = \mathbf{1}$

EXAMPLE 2 $24 \div 4 + 2$

> **SOLUTION:** Divide. $24 \div 4 = 6$
>
> Add. $6 + 2 = \mathbf{8}$

Rule 2: Do the arithmetic inside parentheses first.

EXAMPLE 1 $(21 - 6) \div 3$

> **SOLUTION:** Subtract. $21 - 6 = 15$
>
> Divide. $15 \div 3 = \mathbf{5}$

EXAMPLE 2 $5 \times (4 + 8)$

> **SOLUTION:** Add. $4 + 8 = 12$
>
> Multiply. $5 \times 12 = \mathbf{60}$

Rule 3: Using Rules 1 and 2, start solving arithmetic expressions from the left.

EXAMPLE 1 $20 - 6 + 4$

       SOLUTION: Subtract. $20 - 6 = 14$

                   Add. $14 + 4 = \mathbf{18}$

EXAMPLE 2 $1 + 2 \times 9 \div 6$

       SOLUTION: Multiply. $2 \times 9 = 18$

                   Divide. $18 \div 6 = 3$

                   Add. $1 + 3 = \mathbf{4}$

....

Using the rules for order of operations, evaluate the following arithmetic expressions.

1. $(5 \times 4) - (6 + 3) =$ **2.** $5 \times 4 - 6 + 3 =$

3. $145.6 + 12.2 - 5.7 - 1.1 =$ **4.** $3.2 \times 6 + 7.8 =$

5. $(7.8 + 2.2) \div 5 =$ **6.** $(4 \times 9) \div 3 + 6 =$

7. $4 \times 9 \div 3 + 6 =$ **8.** $1.8 \div 0.02 - 10 - 8 =$

9. $1.8 \div 0.02 - (10 - 8) =$ **10.** $56 - 7 \times 3.5 =$

Using Order of Operations in Combination Word Problems

Look at the following examples to see how to use your knowledge of order of operations to set up a multistep word problem.

EXAMPLE 1 Frank bought dinner for two for $22.50. His bill included a 5% meal tax. What was his total bill?

STEP 1 *question:* What was his total bill?

STEP 2 *solution sentence:*

price of dinner + (5% × price of dinner) = total bill

STEP 3 *set up:*

$22.50 + (0.05 × 22.50) = total bill

STEP 4 *solution:*

Multiply. 0.05 × $22.50 = $1.125

= $1.13 (nearest cent)

Add. $22.50 + $1.13 = **$23.63**

EXAMPLE 2 Eblin lives 19 miles from work. Last week she drove to work and back 5 days and on the weekend drove 170 miles to visit relatives. How many miles did she drive last week commuting and visiting relatives?

STEP 1 *question:* How many miles did she drive?

STEP 2 *solution sentence:*

commuting + visiting relatives = total miles

STEP 3 *set up:*

(19 miles × 5 days × 2 times a day) + 170 miles = total miles

STEP 4 *solution:*

Multiply. 19 × 5 × 2 = 190 miles

Add. 190 miles + 170 miles = **360 miles**

For each word problem, circle the letter of the correct setup.

1. Three friends went out to dinner. Their meal cost $26.88. If they left a tip of $4.00, how much did each person pay if they divided the total amount equally?

   a. ($26.88 ÷ 3) + $4.00
   b. $26.88 + $4.00 ÷ 3
   c. $26.88 + ($4.00 × 3)
   d. ($26.88 + $4.00) ÷ 3
   e. ($26.88 + $4.00) × 3

2. Kathy and Peter went clothes shopping for their baby daughter, Gina. They bought five sleepers for $8.95 each and six T-shirts for $2.40 each. How much money did they spend?

   a. 5 × $8.95 + 6 × $2.40
   b. (5 + $8.95) × (6 + $2.40)
   c. (5 + 6) × ($8.95 + $2.40)
   d. ($8.95 ÷ 5) + ($2.40 × 6)
   e. ($8.95 + $2.40) ÷ (5 + 6)

3. Katrina pays $99.90 for her monthly train pass. If she used her pass twice a day for 23 days last month, what was the average cost of each ride?

   a. ($99.90 ÷ 23) × 2
   b. $99.90 ÷ (23 × 2)
   c. $99.90 − (23 × 2)
   d. $99.90 ÷ 23
   e. $99.90 ÷ 23 × 2

4. A coat normally selling for $80 was marked down 40%. What was the sale price?

   a. $80 − 40
   b. $80 ÷ 40
   c. $80 − 0.40 × $80
   d. $80 + 0.40 × $80
   e. $80 − $80 ÷ 40

5. Dolores needs to buy eggs for the week. She will make six 3-egg omelets for her family. She will also need four eggs for a cake and two eggs for a casserole. How many dozen eggs must she buy?

   a. (6 × 3) + 4 + 2
   b. (6 + 3 + 4 + 2) ÷ 12
   c. 12 × (6 ÷ 3) + (4 ÷ 2)
   d. 6 × 3 ÷ 12 + 4 + 2 ÷ 12
   e. (6 × 3 + 4 + 2) ÷ 12

Using Memory Keys for Multistep Word Problems

Now that you know the order of operations, you can use the memory keys on your calculator for multistep word problems.

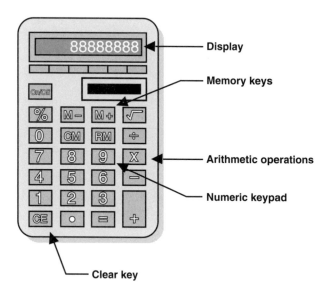

Display

Memory keys

Arithmetic operations

Numeric keypad

Clear key

First you need to write out your setup of the solution of a word problem. Then following the order of operations, do each calculation. You can either add or subtract the result to your calculator memory when you need to. The memory stores these results until it is cleared with either a Clear All or a Clear Memory.

There are some multistep calculations that do not need the memory keys at all, such as a series of multiplications. Practice with your calculator to see if you can find more than one correct procedure for solving a multistep word problem.

Following is an example of how you could use the memory keys to solve a multistep word problem. Since not all calculators handle memory the same way, work through this example on your calculator to make sure these directions work on it.

EXAMPLE   For a party, Hanan bought six bottles of soda for $0.89 each and three bags of chips for $1.49 each. How much did she spend?

STEP 1   Set up the solution.

cost of soda + cost of chips = total cost

$(6 \times 0.89) + (3 \times 1.49) =$ total cost

STEP 2 Key in the first operation in parentheses and add it to memory.

(You may need to use the = key before the memory key.)

You should see 5.34 in your display.

STEP 3 Key in the second operation in parentheses and add it to the amount already in memory.

3 × 1 . 4 9 M+

(You may need to use the = key before the memory key.)

You should see 4.47 in your display.

STEP 4 Press RM (sometimes labeled MRC or RCM) to read the result. You should see 9.81 on the display.

STEP 5 Press CM (Clear Memory) or CA (Clear All) to clear the memory before you start calculating another problem.

For each word problem, look at the solution setup and select the correct question. Then use the setup and your calculator to solve the problem.

1. Sugi has $46 left on her debit card and $48 in cash. She bought $81 in groceries.

   ($46 + $48) − $81

   a. How much more did Sugi have in cash?
   b. How much money did Sugi have left?
   c. How much money did she have before she paid for her groceries?
   d. If she had forgotten her debit card, how many additional dollars would she have needed to pay her bill?
   e. How much money does Sugi need to borrow to pay her bill?

2. Emily mixes a fruit cooler with 5 ounces of fruit juice to 3 ounces of seltzer. For a party she wants to make 2 gallons (164 ounces) of fruit cooler.

$$\frac{5}{5+3} = \frac{n}{256}$$

   a. How much seltzer will she need?
   b. How much more fruit juice than seltzer will she use?
   c. What is the size of one serving?
   d. How many servings is she making?
   e. How much fruit juice will she need?

3. The clearance advertisement said that an additional 20% would be taken off the labeled price at the register. Nerys bought a pair of boots marked $85 and a belt marked $25.

$$\frac{n}{\$85} = \frac{100-20}{100}$$

   a. How much did Nerys save on the boots?
   b. How much did Nerys pay for the boots?
   c. What percent of the original price did Nerys have to pay?
   d. How much did Nerys save on the two items?
   e. How much did Nerys save on the belt?

4. Ultra Clean detergent comes in two sizes. The 64-ounce size costs $8.68. The 32-ounce size costs $4.02.

($8.68 ÷ 64) − ($4.02 ÷ 32)

   a. How much more does the larger size cost?
   b. How much more does the larger size cost per ounce?
   c. What is the per ounce cost of the larger size?
   d. What is the per ounce cost of the smaller size?
   e. How much more detergent is in the larger size?

Using Pictures or Diagrams to Set Up Multistep Word Problems

You can use pictures or diagrams to help you set up and solve multistep word problems.

EXAMPLE 1 Holly just moved into her new studio apartment. The main room is 30 feet long by 15 feet wide, and the bathroom is 9 feet long and 8 feet wide. What is the total size of her apartment in square feet?

   STEP 1 *question:* What is the total size of her apartment?

   STEP 2 *picture:*

   STEP 3 *set up:*

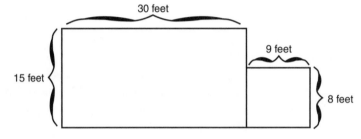

   (30 feet × 15 feet) + (9 feet × 8 feet) = total size

   STEP 4 *solution:*

   Multiply. 30 feet × 15 feet = 450 square feet

   Multiply. 9 feet × 8 feet = 72 square feet

   Add. 450 square feet + 72 square feet = **522 square feet**

EXAMPLE 2 Donna's car gets 27 miles per gallon. After filling her 18-gallon gas tank, she drove 135 miles. How many more miles can she drive before her car runs out of gas?

   STEP 1 *question:* How many more miles?

   STEP 2 *diagram:*

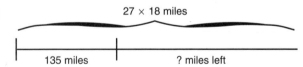

   STEP 3 *set up:*

   (27 mpg × 18 gallons) – 135 miles = miles left

   STEP 4 *solution:*

   Multiply. 27 mpg × 18 gallons = 486 miles

   Subtract. 486 miles – 135 miles = **351 miles**

For each word problem, draw a picture or diagram and circle the letter of the correct setup.

1. A set of silverware included 8 place settings of a knife, fork, salad fork, teaspoon, and soup spoon as well as 6 serving pieces. How many pieces of silverware are in the set:

   a. 8×6 diagram:
   b. $8 \times 6 - 5$
   c. $8 \times 5 + 6$
   d. $5 + 8 \times 6$
   e. $8 \times 6 \div 5$

2. A florist has 420 roses and 380 carnations. How many bouquets, each containing 5 flowers, can be made from these flowers?

   a. $(420 + 380) \times 5$ diagram:
   b. $5 \times 420 - 380$
   c. $5 \div (420 + 380)$
   d. $420 \times 5 - 380 \times 5$
   e. $420 \div 5 + 380 \div 5$

3. Jan turned a 9-foot by 12-foot room in her home into an office. If she wants three equally sized bookcases along each of the 9-foot walls, how wide can each bookcase be?

   a. $(9 \div 3) \times 2$ diagram:
   b. $(9 \times 12) \div 3$
   c. $(9 \div 3) \times 12$
   d. $9 \div 3$
   e. $(12 \div 3) \times 9$

4. The theater has 30 rows of 25 seats each. If 150 of the seats are taken, how many are empty?

   a. $(30 \times 25) - 150$ diagram:
   b. $(30 \times 25) \div 150$
   c. $150 - 30 \times 25$
   d. $(30 + 25) \times 150$
   e. $(150 \div 30) + 25$

Solving Combination Word Problems Involving Conversions

Many combination word problems involve conversions. To solve the following examples and problems, you should refer to the conversion chart on page 188. You should notice that a conversion is needed when one unit of measurement appears in the necessary information and a different unit of measurement is called for in the question.

EXAMPLE 1 A dairy farm sold 156 *quarts* of milk at its own store and shipped out an additional 868 *quarts* to nearby supermarkets. How many *gallons* of milk were marketed?

STEP 1 *question:* How many gallons of milk were marketed?

STEP 2 *necessary information:* 156 quarts, 868 quarts

STEP 3 *solution statement:*

$$\frac{\text{quarts}}{\text{gallon}} = \frac{\text{quarts}}{\text{gallon}}$$

$$\frac{4}{1} = \frac{quarts}{gallons}$$

There are 4 quarts in a gallon. This is written on the left side of the proportion as $\frac{4}{1}$.

$$\frac{4}{1} = \frac{1{,}024}{n}$$

missing information sentence:

quarts + quarts = total quarts

$$4 \times n = 1 \times 1{,}024$$
$$4n = 1{,}024$$

156 + 868 = 1,024 quarts

STEP 4 Solve.

$$n = \frac{1{,}024}{4} = 256 \; gallons$$

EXAMPLE 2 A mill is cutting 8-*foot* lengths of lumber into chair legs. There are 6 *inches* of scrap for each length. What percent of the wood is scrap?

STEP 1 *question:* What percent of the wood is scrap?

STEP 2 *necessary information:* 8-foot, 6 inches

STEP 3 *solution statement:*

$$\frac{\text{part}}{\text{whole}} = \frac{\text{percent}}{100}$$

$$\frac{6 \; inches}{8 \; feet} = \frac{n}{100}$$

Since all the information must be in the same unit of measurement, do the conversion.

conversion:

$$\frac{1 \text{ foot}}{12 \text{ inches}} = \frac{8 \text{ feet}}{x}$$

$$x = 12 \times 8$$

$$x = 96 \text{ inches}$$

> **Note:** In the conversion, the letter x was used to stand for the unknown number of inches. Any letter can be used to stand for an unknown.

STEP 4 Solve.

$$\frac{6 \text{ inches}}{96 \text{ inches}} = \frac{n}{100}$$

$$96n = 6 \times 100$$

$$96n = 600$$

$$n = \frac{600}{96} = 6\frac{1}{4}\%$$

 Solve the following word problems, making the necessary conversions. Be careful; not all problems need a conversion. Refer to the conversion chart on page 188 if necessary.

1. Tile Town sells 81-square-inch tiles. How many tiles are needed to cover a 54-square-foot floor?

2. On the airplane assembly line, Isadore was able to make 20 welds an hour. How many welds did he make during a 9-hour workday?

3. On Interstate Highway, there is a reflector every 528 feet. How many reflectors are there on the stretch of highway shown at the right?

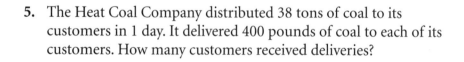

4. The medical center needed 48 gallons of blood after the earthquake. A nearby city donated 26 gallons of blood. The rest was donated at the medical center by people each giving 1 pint of blood. How many people gave a pint of blood at the center?

5. The Heat Coal Company distributed 38 tons of coal to its customers in 1 day. It delivered 400 pounds of coal to each of its customers. How many customers received deliveries?

6. Sharon was able to type 463 numbers during a 5-minute timing for data entry. At this rate, how many numbers could she type in an hour?

7. Lynn brought 12 quarts of ice cream to the Fourth of July picnic. If she gives each person a 4-ounce serving of ice cream, how many people will get the ice cream?

Solving Word Problems Containing Unnecessary Information

Unnecessary information is more difficult to spot in combination word problems than in one-step word problems. The key to identifying unnecessary numbers is in working backward from the question. Once you write a word sentence, look at all the given information, and decide what is needed to answer the question.

EXAMPLE 1   At sunrise the temperature was 54 degrees. By midafternoon, it had risen 27 degrees. The temperature then began falling, until by midnight it had dropped 19 degrees from the high. What was the temperature at midafternoon?

STEP 1   *question:* What was the temperature at midafternoon?

STEP 2   *necessary information:* 54 degrees, 27 degrees (The fact that the temperature had dropped another 19 degrees by midnight is unnecessary information.)

STEP 3   This is a one-step problem. Write a word sentence.
sunrise temperature + change = midafternoon temperature

STEP 4   Solve.

$54 + 27 = $ **81 degrees**

EXAMPLE 2   A 0.8-ounce jar of basil sells for $0.98. Marie has 3.5 pounds of basil to pack into the jars. How many jars will she need?

STEP 1   *question:* How many jars will she need?

STEP 2   *necessary information:* 0.8 ounce, 3.5 pounds

(The cost of the jar of basil is unnecessary information.)

STEP 3   *solution statement:*

$$\frac{\text{total weight}}{\text{number of jars}} = \frac{\text{weight}}{1 \text{ jar}}$$

$$\frac{3.5 \text{ pounds}}{n \text{ jars}} = \frac{0.8 \text{ ounce}}{1 \text{ jar}}$$

Since all your weights must be in the same unit of measurement, your next step must be a conversion to find the number of ounces in a pound.

conversion: $\dfrac{16 \text{ ounces}}{1 \text{ pound}} = \dfrac{n \text{ ounces}}{3.5 \text{ pounds}}$

$$1 \times n = 3.5 \times 16$$
$$n = \textbf{56 ounces}$$

$$\frac{56 \text{ ounces}}{n \text{ jars}} = \frac{0.8 \text{ ounce}}{1 \text{ jar}}$$

$$0.8 \times n = 56 \times 1$$
$$0.8n = 56$$
$$n = \frac{56}{0.8} = 70 \text{ jars}$$

STEP 4   Solve.

Write the word sentences or proportion needed to solve the following word problems. Underline the necessary information. Then solve the problem. Be careful; many of these problems contain unnecessary information.

1. At the beginning of the school year, the Philadelphia school system had 103,912 students. During the course of the year, 4,657 students left the system, while 1,288 more students were enrolled. What was the student population at the end of the year?

2. At the beginning of the school year, the Philadelphia school system had 103,912 students. During the course of the year, 4,657 students left the system, while 1,288 more students were enrolled. How many different students spent at least part of the year in the Philadelphia school system?

3. At sunrise the temperature was 54 degrees. By midafternoon, it had risen 27 degrees. The temperature then began falling, until by midnight it had dropped 19 degrees from the high. What was the temperature at midnight?

4. Every week, after having $153 taken out of his paycheck, Lloyd takes home $348. What was Lloyd's take-home pay for a 52-week year?

5. Ahmed bought three paperbacks and two magazines at the drugstore at the prices shown at the right. He paid for his purchases with a $50 bill. How much change did he receive at the drugstore?

Hoyle's Drugstore	
Newspapers	$0.55
Paperbacks	$6.95
Magazines	$3.50
Postcards	$0.35

6. Sangita is a member of a cooperative grocery store. She gets a 20% discount off everything she buys in the store. She bought a 5-pound bag of oranges marked $2.80. After receiving her discount, how much did she pay for the oranges?

Solving Longer Combination Word Problems

Sometimes word problems cannot be solved by being broken into two one-step problems. Three or more steps may be needed to solve the problem. The method used with these problems is the same as the method used throughout this chapter with combination word problems. Keep working backward from the question. Set up a solution sentence and solve shorter problems to get all of the information that you need.

EXAMPLE   Sylvia went shopping in the bargain basement. She bought a $24.99 dress marked $\frac{1}{3}$ off and a $16.95 pair of pants marked down 20%. How much did she spend?

STEP 1   *question:* How much did she spend?

STEP 2   *necessary information:* $24.99, $\frac{1}{3}$ off; $16.95, marked down 20%

STEP 3   *solution sentence:*

dress price + pants price = total spent

To solve this, you must find the sale prices of both the dress and the pants. Both can be found by using this *missing information* sentence:

original price − discount amount = sale price

You can find the discount by multiplying the original amount by a fraction or percent.

dress

$24.99 − ($\frac{1}{3}$ × 24.99) = sale price
24.99 − 8.33 = $16.66

pants

$16.95 − (20% of 16.95) = sale price
16.95 − (.20 × 16.95) = sale price
16.95 − 3.39 = $13.56

STEP 4   Solve.

$16.66 + $13.56 = **$30.22**

> **Note:** An earlier chapter used the proportion method for solving percent word problems. However, if a problem requires you to find a percent of an amount, there is another method. Simply change the percent to a decimal and multiply. In the example above, 20% was changed to .20.

For every problem, write all necessary word sentences or proportions. Then solve the problem. Round money solutions to the nearest cent.

1. Kerry bought seven apples and a cantaloupe at the prices shown at the right. How much did she spend?

Cantaloupe	$1.88 each
Grapes	$1.69 per pound
Apples	$2.76 per dozen

2. Aaron received a gas bill of $36.80 for 32 gallons of bottled gas. If he pays the bill within 10 days, he will receive a 6% discount. How much will he pay if he pays his bill within 10 days?

3. Harold's doctor advised him to cut down on the calories he consumes by 28%. Harold has been consuming 4,200 calories a day. If Harold's breakfast contains 797 calories, how many calories can he have during the rest of the day?

4. Sarkis is a salesman. He receives a salary of $70 a week plus a 6% commission on all his sales over $200. Last week he sold $4,160 worth of merchandise. What was he paid for the week?

5. Dinora drove 3,627 miles from coast to coast. Her car averaged 31 miles per gallon, and she spent $186 for gas. On the average, what did she pay per gallon of gas?

Solving Combination Word Problems

 In the following problems, choose the one best answer. Round decimals to the nearest cent or the nearest hundredth.

1. Every day Kevin has to drive 7 miles each way to work and back. At work, he has to drive his truck on a 296-mile delivery route. How many miles does he drive during a 5-day workweek?

   a. 310 miles
   b. 315 miles
   c. 1,550 miles
   d. 4,214 miles
   e. none of the above

2. Every day, Jason has a 14-mile round-trip drive to work. He then has to drive his truck on a 296-mile delivery route 5 days a week. How many miles does he drive each day?

   a. 310 miles
   b. 315 miles
   c. 1,550 miles
   d. 4,214 miles
   e. none of the above

3. For his art class, Karl spent $135 on books and $225 on materials. To cover costs, how much did each of his 15 students pay?

   a. $360
   b. $90
   c. $24
   d. $15
   e. $9

4. Jessie's restaurant had four small dining rooms with a capacity of 28 people each and a main dining room with a capacity of 94 people. What was the total capacity of the restaurant?

   a. 126 people
   b. 658 people
   c. 348 people
   d. 122 people
   e. 206 people

5. Each team in the 8-team football league used to have a roster of 36 players. The league decided to decrease each team's roster size by 3 players. Before the change, how many players were in the league?

   a. 180 players
   b. 288 players
   c. 285 players
   d. 264 players
   e. 396 players

6. Each team in the 8-team football league used to have a roster of 36 players. The league decided to decrease each team's roster size by 3 players. After the change, how many players were in the league?

   a. 180 players
   b. 288 players
   c. 285 players
   d. 264 players
   e. 396 players

7. At the supermarket, Monique bought 2.36 pounds of cheese and 4 pounds of apples. What was the total cost of the cheese and apples at the prices shown at the right?

   a. $6.36
   b. $6.09
   c. $3.56
   d. $9.65
   e. $9.44

   **Meg's Market
   On Sale This Week!**

   Apples—only $0.89/pound
   Chicken—only $1.39/pound
   Potato Salad—only $1.29/pint
   Cheese—only $2.58/pound

8. A bottle contains 6 cups of laundry detergent. The directions say to use $\frac{1}{3}$ cup for a top-loading washer and $\frac{1}{4}$ cup for a front-loading washer. How many more loads per bottle can you do with a front-loading washer than with a top-loading washer?

   a. 1 load
   b. 3 loads
   c. 6 loads
   d. 8 loads
   e. 9 loads

Word Problems Posttest A

This posttest gives you a chance to check your skill at solving word problems. Take your time and work each problem carefully. When you finish, check your answers and review any topics on which you need more work. (**Caution:** At least one problem does not contain enough information to solve the problem.)

1. Three tablespoons cocoa plus 1 tablespoon fat can be substituted for 1 ounce chocolate in baking recipes. A recipe for chocolate cake calls for 12 ounces of chocolate. If Shirley is substituting cocoa for chocolate, how much cocoa should she use?

2. Matt has a 400-square-inch board. He needs a 25-square-inch piece of the board for the floor of a birdhouse. What percent of the board will he need for the floor of the birdhouse?

3. There are 5,372 school-age children in town. Of those children, 1,547 either go to private school or have dropped out. How many children remain in the town's public schools?

4. A bushel of apples weighs 48 pounds. Tanya wants to buy 12 pounds of apples. How many bushels should she buy?

5. At the sidewalk stand, Jason bought a hot dog and a soda. How much did he spend at the prices shown at the right?

HOT DOG	1.30
ITALIAN SAUSAGE	1.95
POTATO CHIPS	.50
SODA	.65

HOT DOGS

6. If Kenneth retires at age 65, he will receive as a pension 80% of his salary of $28,657. If he retires at age 62, he will receive only 70% of his salary. How much less will he receive for his pension if he retires early?

7. One cup sugar plus $\frac{1}{4}$ cup liquid can be substituted for 1 cup corn syrup in baking recipes. A recipe calls for $1\frac{1}{2}$ cups corn syrup. If Mira is substituting sugar for corn syrup, how much liquid should she add?

8. A conservation organization charged each member $20 dues plus $15 for the organization's magazine. How much money did the organization collect from its 13,819 members?

9. Pat and Connie are able to put down $16,000 as a down payment on a new home. Their bank told them that they must pay at least 8% of the purchase price as a down payment. What is the most expensive home they can afford?

10. For her wardrobe, Mrs. Are was given a Paris original worth $1,346, a New York original worth $658, and a Goodwill original worth $4. What was the total value of the clothes given to her?

11. After 3 years, Elsie's car had lost $\frac{1}{3}$ of its original value. Two years later, it had lost an additional $\frac{1}{4}$ of its original value. If she bought the car for $9,600, what was its value after 5 years?

12. There are 3 feet in a yard. There are 1,760 yards in a mile. Connie is planning to walk the 5-mile Walk for Peace. How many feet long is the Walk for Peace?

13. Lorraine weighed $172\frac{1}{2}$ pounds. She lost $47\frac{3}{4}$ pounds in one year. What was her new weight?

14. To qualify for the car race, Christine needed to drive 100 miles in under 43 minutes. She completed the first lap in $4\frac{1}{2}$ minutes. At this rate, what will be her total time for the 100-mile qualifying distance?

15. Nickilena, Jean, Rosemary, and Elaine went into business together. The four-woman partnership earned $336,460 and had expenses of $123,188. If they divided the profits equally, how much did each woman make?

16. Sears is offering 20% off on its $260 refrigerator. How much can you save by buying the refrigerator on sale?

17. Before a recent election, $\frac{1}{3}$ of the voters polled said they were planning to vote for the incumbent, while $\frac{1}{4}$ said they were planning to vote for the challenger. The rest were undecided. What fraction of the voters had decided which way they were going to vote?

18. Denise is paid $7.20 per hour at her part-time job. Last week she worked 17.5 hours. How much did she earn last week at her part-time job?

19. Jane bought a new hatchback automobile. She ordered $4,350 of added options and received a $2,650 rebate. How much did Jane pay for the car?

20. East Somerville has 948 homes. The Heart Association has 12 people collecting donations. If they all visit the same number of homes, how many homes should each of them visit?

21. Melvin received an electric bill for $86.29. He knows that it cost him $59.00 a month for his air conditioning. How much would his bill have been if he had not operated the air conditioner?

22. Eileen bought three pairs of socks for $1.79 each and four towels for $2.69 each. How much did she spend?

23. Steve's Ice Cream Store puts $\frac{1}{16}$ pound of whipped cream on every sundae. For how many sundaes will the container of whipped cream pictured at the right last?

24. After paying $24.43 for dinner and $7.50 for a movie, Florence paid the baby-sitter $20.00. How much did the evening cost her?

25. A pile of books weighed 34.2 pounds. If each book weighed 0.6 pound, how many books were in the pile?

Word Problems Posttest A Prescriptions

Circle the number of any problem that you miss. A passing score is 20 correct answers. If you passed the test, go on to Using Number Power. If you did not pass the test, review the chapters in this book or refer to these practice pages in other materials from Contemporary Books.

PROBLEM NUMBERS	PRESCRIPTION MATERIALS	PRACTICE PAGES
1, 3, 10, 20	whole numbers	18–39, 61–76
	Math Exercises: Whole Numbers and Money	3–29
	Real Numbers: Estimation 1	5–36
	Breakthroughs in Math: Book 1	7–133
4, 7, 13, 17, 23	fractions	52–60, 80–88
	Math Exercises: Fractions	3–29
	Real Numbers: Estimation 2	1–38
	Math Skills That Work: Book 2	70–105
	Breakthroughs in Math: Book 2	66–113
5, 18, 21, 24, 25	decimals	40–51, 56–60, 77–79, 87–88
	Math Exercises: Decimals	3–29
	Real Numbers: Estimation 1	37–64
	Math Skills That Work: Book 2	32–69
	Breakthroughs in Math: Book 2	34–65
2, 9, 16	percents	118–136
	Math Exercises: Percents	3–29
	Real Numbers: Estimation 2	39–64
	Math Skills That Work: Book 2	106–139
	Breakthroughs in Math: Book 2	114–141
12	conversion	100–101, 154–155
	Math Exercises: Measurement	6–24
	Breakthroughs in Math: Book 1	134–152
14, 19	not enough information	110–114
	Math Exercises: Problem Solving and Applications	18–23
6, 8, 11, 15, 22	multistep word problems	137–161
	Math Exercises: Problem Solving and Applications	3–16

Word Problems Posttest B

This test has a multiple-choice format much like many standardized tests. Take your time and work each problem carefully. Round decimals to the nearest cent or the nearest hundredth. Circle the correct answer to each problem.

1. Large eggs weigh $1\frac{1}{2}$ pounds per dozen. Dawn bought eight large eggs. How much did the eggs weigh?

   a. 3 ounces
   b. $\frac{1}{3}$ pound
   c. 1 pound
   d. 18 ounces
   e. not enough information given

2. Glenn, the owner of a hardware store, originally paid $540.60 for 15 tool sets. At his year-end clearance sale, he sold the last tool set for $24.00. How much money did he lose on the last tool set?

   a. $180.60
   b. $1.50
   c. $12.04
   d. $36.04
   e. none of the above

3. Manny was working as a hot dog vendor. He sold a total of 426 hot dogs in one weekend. If he sold 198 on Saturday, how many did he sell on Sunday?

   a. 624 hot dogs
   b. 332 hot dogs
   c. 228 hot dogs
   d. 514 hot dogs
   e. none of the above

4. The television announcer reported that Elizabeth Quezada had received 39% of the votes in the race for mayor. The totals board behind the announcer showed that Elizabeth had received 156,000 votes. How many votes were cast in the election?

   a. 40,000 votes
   b. 400,000 votes
   c. 156,039 votes
   d. 608,480 votes
   e. 60,840 votes

5. On the average, Morriston Airport has 96 jumbo jets arriving each day. Each jumbo jet has an average of 214 passengers. How many passengers arrive by jumbo jet at Kennedy Airport each day?

   a. 310 passengers
   b. 20,544 passengers
   c. 118 passengers
   d. 222 passengers
   e. none of the above

6. To finish off the room, Ed needs a tile only $\frac{1}{3}$ foot wide. How much did he have to cut off the tile pictured at the right so that it would fit?

   a. $\frac{1}{2}$ foot
   b. $\frac{5}{12}$ foot
   c. $\frac{4}{7}$ foot
   d. $\frac{1}{4}$ foot
   e. $\frac{4}{9}$ foot

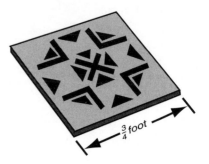

$\frac{3}{4}$ foot

7. After picking a bushel of apples, Tina planned to divide the apples equally among herself and five of her neighbors. How many apples did each of them get if the bushel weighed 54 pounds?

   a. 9 apples
   b. 60 apples
   c. 48 apples
   d. 324 apples
   e. not enough information given

8. Monty uses 1.23 cubic yards of concrete to cover 100 square feet with 4 inches of concrete. How many cubic yards does he need to cover 550 square feet with 4 inches of concrete?

   a. 650 square feet
   b. 4.92 cubic yards
   c. 6.77 cubic yards
   d. 2,200 square inches
   e. 27.06 cubic yards

9. Pedro needs 4 pounds of hamburger for his chili recipe. In his freezer, he has a 2.64-pound package of hamburger. How much more hamburger does he need?

   a. 6.64 pounds
   b. 2.68 pounds
   c. 1.36 pounds
   d. 1.52 pounds
   e. 10.56 pounds

10. Last year the city's supermarkets sold 1,638,000 gallons of milk. There are 78,000 people in the city. On the average, how many gallons of milk did each person buy?

   a. 1,716,000 gallons
   b. 1,560,000 gallons
   c. 21 gallons
   d. 127,716 million gallons
   e. not enough information given

11. After having $98.23 taken out of his paycheck, Maurice takes home $332.77 every week. What are Maurice's total gross earnings for a 52-week year?

   a. $12,196.08
   b. $22,412.00
   c. $431.00
   d. $17,304.04
   e. $5,107.96

12. In the last year 423 service stations in the state closed. Only 2,135 remain. How many service stations existed in the state a year ago?

   a. 2,558 service stations
   b. 1,712 service stations
   c. 2,312 service stations
   d. 2,512 service stations
   e. none of the above

13. A two-thirds majority of those voting in the House of Representatives is needed to override a presidential veto. If all 435 representatives vote, how many votes are needed to override a veto?

   a. 290 votes
   b. 145 votes
   c. 657 votes
   d. 658 votes
   e. 224 votes

14. Naomi had $61 in her checking account. She wrote a check for $28 and made a deposit. How much money did she then have in the account?

   a. $89
   b. $33
   c. $2.18
   d. $1708
   e. not enough information given

15. Avi needed to replace the molding on the left side of his car after it was damaged. The door needed $33\frac{3}{4}$ inches of molding, while the rear quarter panel needed $51\frac{2}{3}$ inches. How many inches of molding did he need if he replaced the molding on the door and the rear quarter panel?

   a. $2,247\frac{5}{12}$ inches
   b. $85\frac{5}{12}$ inches
   c. $17\frac{11}{12}$ inches
   d. $\frac{87}{124}$ inches
   e. $\frac{124}{87}$ inches

16. Ben, who works at the meat counter at the local supermarket, had to price the meat yesterday because the machine that normally did the job was broken. What price should he put on a 2.64-pound rib roast selling at $3.96 a pound?

   a. $1.50
   b. $5.94
   c. $6.60
   d. $10.45
   e. $1.32

17. At the factory, 28% of the workers were women. There were 432 male workers. What was the total number of workers at the factory?

   a. 460 workers

   b. 12,096 workers

   c. 600 workers

   d. 1,543 workers

   e. 404 workers

18. Sarah bought the carton of nails pictured at the right. How much did each nail weigh?

   a. 56 pounds

   b. 100 pounds

   c. 0.01 pound

   d. $\frac{1}{56}$ pound

   e. $\frac{3}{100}$ pound

19. In the first quarter, the Philadelphia 76ers hit only 7 out of 25 field goal attempts. What was their scoring percentage?

   a. 28%

   b. 32%

   c. 72%

   d. 76%

   e. 18%

20. Carla gained 3 pounds in the first month of her new diet and 4 pounds in the second month. Her original weight was 104 pounds. What was her new weight?

   a. 97 pounds

   b. 105 pounds

   c. 103 pounds

   d. 111 pounds

   e. 100 pounds

21. Peg bought the roast and the steak shown at the right. How much meat did she buy?

1.23 pound steak

3.69 pound roast

   a. 4.92 pounds

   b. 3 pounds

   c. 4.54 pounds

   d. 2.46 pounds

   e. 0.33 pound

22. Glennie had $74.81 in her checking account. She wrote checks for $46.19 and $22.45. She then made a $60.00 deposit. What was her new balance?

    a. $203.45
    b. $66.17
    c. $83.45
    d. $53.83
    e. $38.55

23. Premium Ice Cream is 9% milkfat. How many pounds of milkfat are in a 450-pound batch of Premium Ice Cream?

    a. 50 pounds
    b. 441 pounds
    c. 459 pounds
    d. 40.5 pounds
    e. 2 pounds

24. At the start of a trip, Tony filled his gas tank. After driving 168 miles, he needed 5.6 gallons of gasoline to fill his tank. How many gallons of gasoline would he use for the 417-mile drive from his home to his brother's home?

    a. 44.5 gallons
    b. 13.9 gallons
    c. 74.5 gallons
    d. 8.3 gallons
    e. 19.5 gallons

25. A piece of cheese was labeled $1.79 a pound. The price of the cheese was $1.06. How much did the cheese weigh?

    a. $2.85
    b. $0.73
    c. 1.69 pounds
    d. 1.90 pounds
    e. 0.59 pound

Word Problems Posttest B Chart

If you missed more than one problem on any group below, review the practice pages for those problems. Then redo the problems you got wrong before going on to Using Number Power. If you had a passing score, redo any problem you missed and go on to Using Number Power on page 175.

PROBLEM NUMBERS	SKILL AREA	PRACTICE PAGES
3, 12, 20	add or subtract whole numbers	18–39
5, 10	multiply or divide whole numbers	61–76
6, 15	add or subtract fractions	52–60
13, 18	multiply or divide fractions	80–88
9, 21	add or subtract decimals	40–51, 56–60
16, 25	multiply or divide decimals	77–79, 87–88
4, 19, 23	percents	118–136
1	conversion	100–101, 154–155
7, 14	not enough information	110–114
2, 8, 11, 17, 22, 24	multistep word problems	137–161

Using
Number
Power

Using Information from a Chart

Even a relatively small chart can contain a great amount of useful information. Sometimes you will need to use your problem-solving and math skills to understand and utilize the information contained in a chart.

	Chart of Beverages				
Serving Size	Beverage	Calories	Carbohydrates	Protein	Fat
8 ounces	2% lowfat milk	113 cal	11 grams	7 grams	4 grams
12 ounces	vanilla milk shake	381 cal	60 grams	13 grams	10 grams
8 ounces	orange juice from concentrate	91 cal	22 grams	1 gram	0 gram
12 ounces	cola	133 cal	34 grams	0 gram	0 gram

Georgiana wanted to gain weight. How many more calories would she get from a 12-ounce serving of the highest calorie beverage compared to a 12-ounce serving of the next highest calorie beverage?

At first glance, you might think that the cola is the next highest calorie beverage, but the serving size is larger than the milk or the orange juice. Since the milk and the orange juice are both 8-ounce servings and the milk is higher in calories, you can eliminate the juice. You can now set up a proportion to find the calories in a 12-ounce serving of low-fat milk.

$$\frac{8 \text{ ounces}}{12 \text{ ounces}} = \frac{113 \text{ calories}}{n \text{ calories}}$$

$8n = 1{,}356$

$n = $ **169.5 calories** in 12 ounces of milk

So 12 ounces of milk is the next highest calorie beverage.

Highest calorie beverage – next highest calorie beverage = difference in calories

381 calories – 169.5 calories = **211.5 calories**

Use the chart of beverages to solve the following word problems.

1. For breakfast Danielle had an 8-ounce glass of orange juice. At lunch she had a 12-ounce milk shake, and for dinner she drank a 12-ounce bottle of cola. How many grams of carbohydrates did she get from beverages at the three meals?

   a. 32 grams
   b. 38 grams
   c. 116 grams
   d. 127 grams
   e. 505 grams

2. Keion had an 18-ounce vanilla milk shake. How many grams of fat were in his milk shake?

   a. 10 ounces
   b. 12 ounces
   c. 13 ounces
   d. 15 ounces
   e. 16 ounces

Use the nutrition chart to solve the following word problems.

	Calories	Carbohydrates	Protein	Fat
12-ounce sirloin steak	914	0 g	94 g	57 g
5-ounce hamburger on bun	405	24 g	27 g	21 g
6-ounce fried chicken breast	442	15 g	42 g	22 g
10-ounce spaghetti with tomato sauce	246	52 g	8 g	1 g
8-ounce broiled salmon	412	0 g	61 g	17 g

3. When Jean looked at the nutrition chart, she had trouble comparing the different main dishes because the portions were different sizes. She was trying to decide whether to make a 12-ounce portion of sirloin steak or a 12-ounce portion of broiled salmon. How many more calories was the steak than the salmon?

   a. 914 calories
   b. 1,326 calories
   c. 502 calories
   d. 296 calories
   e. 1,532 calories

4. Elba wanted to prepare a main dish that was approximately 600 calories. If she prepared one of the main dishes from the chart, how large should a portion of that main dish be?

5. Max was going to have a 10-ounce portion of sirloin steak, but then decided he needed to cut down on the amount of fat in his diet. How much less fat would he eat if he instead had a 10-ounce portion of one of the other main dishes on the chart?

6. Using the chart as a guide, where does the grams of carbohydrates in a hamburger on bun come from, the hamburger or the bun or both?

7. Emily decided she needed more protein in her diet. She also wanted to have less fat in her diet. Which entrée would be the best choice for her?

   a. sirloin steak
   b. hamburger on bun
   c. fried chicken breast
   d. spaghetti with tomato sauce
   e. broiled salmon

Use the exercise chart to answer the following questions.

Exercise for a 130-Pound Woman

Walking 3 mph	5 calories/minute
Jogging 5.5 mph	10 calories/minute
Running 10 mph	19 calories/minute
Swimming 25 yd/min	4 calories/minute
Bicycling 6 mph	4 calories/minute
Tennis singles	6 calories/minute
Cross-country skiing	6 calories/minute
Aerobic dancing	8 calories/minute
Recreational volleyball	3 calories/minute
Sleeping	1 calorie/minute

Match questions 8 through 10 to the correct solutions listed below.
Some questions have more than one solution.

a. recreational volleyball for 90 minutes + tennis for 55 minutes

b. running for 25 minutes + walking for 45 minutes + bicycling for 25 minutes

c. jogging for 40 minutes + swimming for 30 minutes + bicycling for 2 hours

d. aerobic dancing for 40 minutes + tennis for 40 minutes + jogging for 24 minutes

e. cross-country skiing for 2 hours + aerobic dancing for 35 minutes

8. How could Fernande burn 1,000 calories? _____

9. Rafaela wanted to spend no more than 2 hours doing at least three different activities burning a total of 800 calories. How could she do it? _____

10. Juliette wanted to burn 600 calories while exercising at least 2 hours. How could she do it? _____

11. Design a fitness program for yourself using the numbers from the table (even if you are not a 130-pound woman). Plan to burn exactly 500 calories in at least an hour of activity.

12. Design an exercise program that is exactly one hour long and consists of at least two different activities. How many calories would a 130-pound woman burn if she followed your exercise program?

Challenging Word Problems

Sometimes word problems require more than translating words into mathematics. You might have to do more complex problem solving.

EXAMPLE   Juana's recipe for chili calls for 2 teaspoons of hot sauce per gallon. Unfortunately, she misread the instructions and put in 2 tablespoons of hot sauce. How much more chili should she make in order to readjust her chili back to the recipe?

STEP 1   *question:* How much more chili should she make in order to readjust her chili back to the recipe?

STEP 2   *necessary information:* 2 teaspoons per gallon, 2 tablespoons

STEP 3   Decide what arithmetic operation to use. Convert tablespoons to teaspoons. Then use a proportion to find the total amount of chili.

Final equation: total amount of chili – chili already made = additional chili

STEP 4   There are 3 teaspoons in a tablespoon.

$$\frac{3 \text{ teaspoons}}{1 \text{ tablespoon}} = \frac{n \text{ teaspoons}}{2 \text{ tablespoons}}$$

$$n = 6 \text{ teaspoons}$$

STEP 5   Calculate the new total amount of chili.

$$\frac{2 \text{ teaspoons}}{1 \text{ gallon}} = \frac{6 \text{ teaspoons}}{x \text{ gallons}}$$

$$2x = 6$$

$$x = 3 \text{ gallons}$$

STEP 6   Calculate how much more chili needs to be made.

1 gallon chili + g gallons to be made = 3 gallons of chili

$g = 2$ gallons of chili

STEP 7   Does the answer make sense?

If three times the original amount of hot sauce is added to the recipe, you should end up with three times the original amount of chili. You will have correctly readjusted the recipe.

Solve the following word problems.

1. After a large storm, Pablo had 8 inches of water in his 30-foot by 40-foot basement. His sump pump pumped out 200 cubic feet of water an hour. Assuming no more water seeped into the basement, how long would it take to pump all the water out of the basement?

2. The same storm left 9 inches of water in Chantel's 30-foot by 50-foot basement, and some water continued to seep in for 4 hours. Her sump pump pumped out 300 cubic feet of water an hour. It took 6 hours to pump the water out of her basement. How much water seeped into the basement?

3. Awilda needs to get gas for her car, buy groceries, shop for a blouse at the department store, take out a book from library, and return a video to the video store. According to the map, what is the shortest total distance she will have to drive to do all her chores and return home?

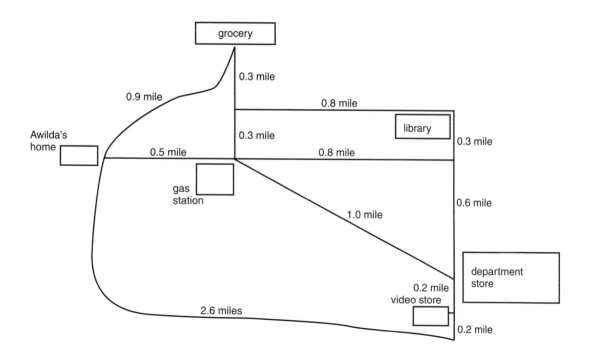

4. It takes 5 seconds for the sound of thunder to travel one mile. Light travels so fast that we can assume we are seeing lightning instantly. A storm is rapidly approaching. Domingo sees a lightning flash and hears the thunder 15 seconds later. Ten minutes later he sees another lightning flash and hears thunder 10 seconds later. If the storm continues to move at the same rate, how long will it take before it is directly overhead?

5. John is designing a 400-square-foot garden. He wants the garden to have the smallest possible perimeter, so he can spend as little as possible on fencing. What should the dimensions of his garden be?

6. Cammy has 100 feet of fencing for a running area for her dog. The run has to be at least 3 feet wide. How long could the run be?

7. Pitcher Randy Johnson can throw a fastball 95 miles per hour. It is 60.5 feet from the rubber at the top of the pitcher's mound to home plate. How long does it take Randy Johnson's fastball to travel from the pitcher's mound to home plate?

Using a Calculator

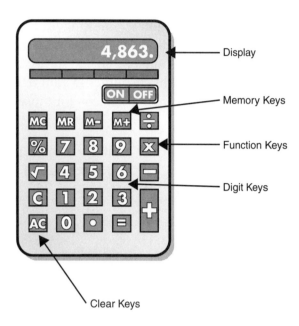

Display

Memory Keys

Function Keys

Digit Keys

Clear Keys

The calculator is an inexpensive convenient tool that you can use to help you with computation. Every calculator has a numeric keypad, keys for the four operations (+ for addition, − for subtraction, × for multiplication, and ÷ or / for division), an equal (=) key, and a clear (C) key. Most calculators also have keys for clear all (AC), percent (%), and square root (√). They may also have keys for the memory functions: memory add (M+), memory subtract (M−), memory read (MR), and memory clear (MC).

If you have never used a calculator before, you should begin by using it to add, subtract, multiply, and divide. Before you use a calculator, you should estimate what you expect your answer to be. If you do a good job of estimating, you should be able to recognize errors caused by accidentally hitting the wrong key on the calculator.

To add, subtract, multiply, or divide two numbers, follow this procedure.
Key in the first number.
Key in the operation (+ , −, ×, ÷).
Key in the second number.
Press the equal sign (=).
The answer should appear in the display.

EXAMPLE   Multiply 48 × 396.

Key in 48 (First press 4 and then press 8.) 4 8

Key in ×. ×

Key in 396 (First press 3, then press 9, and then press 6.) 3 9 6

Press =. =

Look at the display. It should read 19,008. 19,008.

Using Mental Math

Once you decide whether you need to add, subtract, multiply, or divide to solve a word problem, see if you might be able to solve the problem using mental math, or doing the math in your head. If you know your math facts, you should be able to solve a number of problems in this book, as well as many math problems you might encounter in your daily life, by using mental math. Throughout this book, you'll see the mental math icon for those problems you should try to solve using mental math.

The key to mental math is the basic addition and multiplication facts in these tables.

+	1	2	3	4	5	6	7	8	9
1	2	3	4	5	6	7	8	9	10
2	3	4	5	6	7	8	9	10	11
3	4	5	6	7	8	9	10	11	12
4	5	6	7	8	9	10	11	12	13
5	6	7	8	9	10	11	12	13	14
6	7	8	9	10	11	12	13	14	15
7	8	9	10	11	12	13	14	15	16
8	9	10	11	12	13	14	15	16	17
9	10	11	12	13	14	15	16	17	18

×	1	2	3	4	5	6	7	8	9
1	1	2	3	4	5	6	7	8	9
2	2	4	6	8	10	12	14	16	18
3	3	6	9	12	15	18	21	24	27
4	4	8	12	16	20	24	28	32	36
5	5	10	15	20	25	30	35	40	45
6	6	12	18	24	30	36	42	48	54
7	7	14	21	28	35	42	49	56	63
8	8	16	24	32	40	48	56	64	72
9	9	18	27	36	45	54	63	72	81

For example, you can use the table to find 3×4. You can use the same table to find $12 \div 3$.

×	1	2	③	4
1	1	2	3	4
2	2	4	6	8
3	3	6	9	12
④	4	8	⑫	16
5	5	10	15	20

The more you use these math arithmetic facts, the more likely you will be able to memorize them. You could also use flash cards to help with your memorization.

Keep these tables face down when you are doing calculations. If you are not sure of a math fact, write down a guess and turn over the table to see how close your guess was. Using mental math is a skill that you can improve if you are willing to try to use it often.

Using Estimation

An estimate is an approximate answer. Estimation is one of the best ways to figure out whether or not your calculations make any sense. You can estimate either before or after you do a calculation. Many times a good estimate is accurate enough for your purposes and you will have no need to do an exact calculation at all.

Use Common Sense

Use your own knowledge and common sense to make estimates. If you fill a shopping cart full of groceries, will your bill be about $1, $10, $100, or $1,000? Without even knowing what items were purchased, you should be able to estimate that the cart full of groceries would cost closer to $100 than the other choices.

Use Rounded Numbers

When you are given numbers in a word problem, use rounded numbers to make an estimate. For example, gasoline costs $1.199 per gallon and you fill your gas tank with 15.121 gallons. You can round $1.199 to $1.20 and round 15.121 to 15. Then estimate the total cost by multiplying $1.20 by 15 to get an estimate of $18. You would expect the total cost of gasoline to cost about $18.

Use Friendly Numbers

You will often have situations in real life where exact math is not necessary. If you know your basic math facts, you can estimate by using friendly numbers—numbers that are close to the real numbers but that come out evenly. You will not get an exact answer, but you will get a result that is close enough for your purposes. For example, suppose you are in a grocery store and want to get the best buy on cereal. A 12-ounce box costs $2.29, while an 18-ounce box costs $2.99. If you round $2.29 to $2.40 (because 24 can be divided easily by 12), you can see that the 12-ounce box costs a little less than 20 cents an ounce. If you multiply 20 cents × 18 ounces, you get $3.60, much more than the $2.99 cost of the 18-ounce box. You can determine that the 18-ounce box is the better buy.

Develop your estimation skills by first estimating and then doing the exact calculations. The goal in estimating is not to be exact but to be close enough for your needs.

Formulas

PERIMETER

Figure	Name	Formula	Meaning
w *l*	Rectangle	$P = 2l + 2w$	l = length w = width
s	Square	$P = 4s$	s = side

AREA

Figure	Name	Formula	Meaning
w *l*	Rectangle	$A = lw$	l = length w = width
s	Square	$A = s^2$	s = side

VOLUME

Figure	Name	Formula	Meaning
h *w* *l*	Rectangular solid	$V = lwh$	l = length w = width h = height
s	Cube	$V = s^3$	s = side

CONVERSIONS

Time

365 days = 1 year
12 months = 1 year
52 weeks = 1 year
7 days = 1 week
24 hours = 1 day
60 minutes = 1 hour
60 seconds = 1 minute

Length and Area

5,280 feet = 1 mile
1,760 yards = 1 mile
3 feet = 1 yard
36 inches = 1 yard
12 inches = 1 foot
144 square inches = 1 square foot
4,840 square yards = 1 acre
1,000 meters = 1 kilometer
100 centimeters = 1 meter
1,000 millimeters = 1 meter
10 millimeters = 1 centimeter

Weight

2,000 pounds = 1 ton
16 ounces = 1 pound
1,000 grams = 1 kilogram
1,000 milligrams = 1 gram

Volume

4 quarts = 1 gallon
2 pints = 1 quart
4 cups = 1 quart
2 cups = 1 pint
32 ounces = 1 quart
16 ounces = 1 pint
8 ounces = 1 cup
1,000 milliliters = 1 liter

Metric to Customary

1 kilometer = .62 mile
1 meter = 39.37 inches
1 centimeter = .39 inch
1 liter = 1.057 quarts
1 kilogram = 2.2 pounds
1 gram = .035 ounce

Glossary

A

approximation An estimate that is close to a given number, but not exact. A bag of fruit marked $2.89 will cost approximately $3.00.

arithmetic operations Addition, subtraction, multiplication, and division.

C

combination word problem A word problem that needs 2 or more steps to be solved.

conversion Changing from one type of measurement to another. 12 inches = 1 foot.

D

denominator The bottom number of a fraction. In the fraction $\frac{1}{2}$, 2 is the denominator.

diagram A picture or visual aid that helps you understand a word problem.

E

estimation An approximate amount used to determine the accuracy of the arithmetic, or used to give an idea of the answer before doing the arithmetic. 17 + 52 can be rounded to 20 + 50 so the estimation is 70.

F

formula An equation that states a rule or factual information that can be used to solve a certain type of problem. $A = lw$ is the formula for finding the area of a rectangle.

G

given information All the numbers and labels that are in the word problem.

K

key word A clue that can help you decide which arithmetic operation to use. In the problem, find the difference between 15 and 6, the key word *difference* helps you decide to subtract.

L

label The noun (word or symbol) that a number refers to. If you are adding 6 apples and 5 apples, the total amount will be 11 and the label will be apples.

M

math intuition A general understanding of numbers, math operations, and a feel for what a solution should be.

mental math Arithmetic operations that can be done in your head, without the use of pencil and paper or calculator.

N

necessary information The numbers and labels in a word problem that are needed to find a solution.

number sentence A restatement of a word problem as an equation using numbers and labels. In the problem, find the total amount spent for lunch if Jody spent $4.29 and Doretha spent $6.45, the number sentence would be $4.29 + $6.45 = total $ for lunch.

numerator The top number of a fraction. In the fraction $\frac{3}{4}$, 3 is the numerator.

O

order of operations Rules that govern the sequence when you must use more than one arithmetic operation. Order of operations: do arithmetic in parentheses first; do multiplication and division before addition and subtraction; solve from left to right.

P

part A piece that is being compared to a whole.

percent A part of a hundred.

percent circle A memory aid used to help solve percent problems.

proportion A math equation that states that two ratios are equal. $\frac{2}{4} = \frac{1}{2}$ is a proportion.

Q

question The part of a word problem that tells you what to look for.

R

ratio A comparison of the relative size of two groups. The ratio for 3 teachers working with 15 students is 3 teachers/15 students.

restating a problem Saying a problem in your own words to help understand what the problem is asking.

round Estimate to a particular place value. The number 779 rounded to the nearest hundred is 800; rounded to the nearest ten is 780.

S

solution A number and label that will correctly answer the question.

solve To find the solution.

substitution Temporarily replacing a difficult-to-understand number with a small whole number that is easier to picture.

W

word problem A sentence or group of sentences that tells a story, contains numbers, and asks the reader to find another number.

whole A complete amount; in percent, the base for comparison.

Index